Christophe Tarkos:
Ma Langue est Poétique–
Selected Work

Christophe Tarkos:
Ma Langue est Poétique–
Selected Work

ROOF BOOKS
NEW YORK

Acknowledgements:
"The Book of Squares of Earth" was published as pages 52 to 59 in *Christophe Tarkos Les Contemporains Favoris 7*. Collection Morceaux Choisis. Editor: Didier Moulinier. Association "Les Contemporains," 62000 Arras, France 1995.
Toto was published by Encyclopédie des images, Bagneux, France 1997. It also appears in *Pan*, P.O.L., 2000, pages 53 to 79. © P.O.L Éditeur 2000.
"Boxes" was published as *Caisses* by P.O.L. 1998. Excerpted pages: 20, 26, 36, 49. © P.O.L Éditeur 2000.
"Words Do Not Exist" was published as "Les mots n'existent pas," in *Le Signe =*. Paris: P.O.L. pages 28 to 32. © P.O.L Éditeur 1999.
Give is a translation of pages 12 to 19 and page 37 of Volume III *Donne* of the boxed set *Ma langue*. © Al Dante 2000.
"The Train" was originally published as Le Train by Station Underground d'Émerveillement Littéraire 1997. Republished in *Pan*, Paris: P.O.L, 2000; translated excerpts: pages 238 to 242. © P.O.L Éditeur 2000.
Flour originally appeared as *Farine*, published by AIOU.
"Process" is a translation from Processe, Éditions Ulysse Fin de Siècle. © Christophe Tarkos and Ulysse Fin de Siécle 1997.
"hurt" was originally published as "Le mal," pages 19 to 27 of *La Cage*. Music by Eryck Abecassis, Thierry Aué and Clara Mada. Al Dante 2000.
"Two Born," appeared as "Deux nés," pages 19 to 27 in the review *Tombe Tout Court (TTC)*, Tarkos & Compagnie issue 1997.

Cet ouvrage publié dans le cadre du programme d'aide à la publication bénéficie du soutien du Ministère des Affaires Etrangères et du Service Culturel de l'Ambassade de France représenté aux Etats-Unis.
This work, published as part of the program of aid for publication, received support from the French Ministry of Foreign Affairs and the Cultural Service of the French Embassy in the United States.

 This book was made possible, in part, by a grant from the New York NYSCA State Council on the Arts.

ROOF BOOKS
are published by
Segue Foundation
303 East 8th Street
New York, NY 10009
www.segue.org

CONTENTS

INTRODUCTION

1. Tarkos Currents

In 1994 Stacy Doris invited Christophe Tarkos and five other poets who had not yet published a book to contribute twenty pages each for a volume to be published by Fourbis. At this writing all of these poets have had at least one book appear, or are about to.[1] Tarkos (as he is usually referred to) has published at least 25 books.

Tarkos' copiousness has had its effects on the French literary scene because he is such a strong presence, and not merely by volume alone! He is a qualitative and quantitative force, and is seen and heard as much as anyone. Poetry readings are less frequent in France than in North America, with a different ambiance; there are probably not as many readings in the country in a year as there are in a week in New York. It is as likely as not that the rare poetry series in a bar or a series at a poetry center would be organized with actors who declaim others' poetry, old and new, and have few pretensions to any other sort of literary activity. Readings are sometimes organized within institutionalized contexts and on the occasion of new issues of magazines or books. Examining Tarkos' career one finds a sort of evidence that the relation to poetry readings which in English language cultures affects community connections among poets and audiences while providing complementary clues for the reading or reception of works develops with a closer connection to more traditional performance values in France. This tendency emerges in Tarkos' writing in affinities to other art forms.

Tarkos' opus has flourished under present conditions and he has expanded expectations for poetry. Reading or executing live improvisations before a public or on the radio, collaborating on operas, traveling to poetry festivals and events throughout Europe and elsewhere, he excels in, is sought after by and relishes the variety of venues available. His poetry actualizes contrasting currents. While involved in a reinvigoration of the "performative," the work at the same time demonstrates a faith and confidence in traditional capacities of poetry in French. These lead to Mallarmean tendencies as he refers to the "sublime," "magic" and "breath." He has written innumerable poems as well as manifestos of poetry which often couple these aspects with down to earth struggles of existence and social concerns. This combination makes for a poetics whose

7

apparent flattening of language offers incessant poems as self-authentifying systems that gather strength from repetition and concentration, elaborating across mundane events or particular objects.

Contemporary poets find energy and a model in his method, delivery and poetics. Vincent Tholomé, Charles Pennequin, Nathalie Quintane and Kati Molnár have been close in aesthetic and political approaches. These four all perhaps share different means of expressing the third current in Tarkos as a *"poésie prolétaire."*[2] Tarkos has founded or co-founded several reviews, often in collaboration with these poets: *R.R.* (with contributions from Nathalie Quintane), *Facial* (with Charles Pennequin), *Poézi Prolétèr* (with Kati Molnár and Pascal Doury), and Quaderno (with Philippe Beck).

2. Performing Words as Rhythm

My first impression of Tarkos' poetics was that he manages to make words into rhythm:

> I can speak myself, I'm allowed to speak myself, it's permitted, I don't speak myself but I'm allowed, it's not not permitted to speak oneself. . . (*Je peux me parler*)

> Once the motor's running, running turn rage rant fart beat hum gather motor's energy route, Homage to Energy ready go carry off oiled started specific turn gather, homage to getting going. . . ("Nappe")

Like a Philip Glass or Steve Reich composition, there is always much repetition and incremental variation.

> You're ok. You're there. Infinite space doesn't surround you. You're well dressed. You're good looking. You're on site. You're ok. You're there. You're you. You catch yourself, you're not everywhere. You dissolve into you. You don't disappear. . . ("TU ES TOI," *R.R. 52*)

> A halo, an aureole, a verge, a radiation, a dawn, the first dawn, a border, the border, the border that borders, the border that curves, the curve of the border, a halo, a slight light, a taint. . . (*Caisses*)

8

From the link, from the glue, from what holds together, from what
makes the link, from what makes the pliable, from what makes the
bridge, a fastening, from what links, from what isn't left alone, that
makes a group, that makes a link, that makes a sticking link, getting
to the matter, from the fact of having gotten to the matter already,
from having been already stuck. . . ("le lien," *Le signe* =)

The words in Tarkos' writing often have no more than two or three sylla-
bles and, surprisingly, when translating his work, one encounters the
inverse of a nearly universal eventuality of translating from French to
English. Typically words with Anglo Saxon and other origins that are sig-
nificantly shorter than the Latinate French originals present themselves to
the translator. Translating Tarkos one finds that Latinate words in English
which may pertain sabotage the effect that is so much a part of his process.
The argument can be made that the relative scarcity of multi-syllable
words renders Tarkos' writing more accentual than syllabic; somehow
more akin to English language metrics than to French. Certainly the for-
mal constraints of traditional French syllabic verse appear only obliquely,
or at best can be considered as echoes or analogues in completely other
formal aspects, such as the size or shape of a line, "block" "bar," "box"
(Tarkos' usual forms), or circle.[3] In any event, syllable count is further
from the process and effects than the play and movement produced not
exactly by the rhythm of syllables but by the cadence, modulation and
recurrence of word groups and very frequently of shorter words.

Since at least the late 1940s sound poets have been engaged in a vari-
ety of poetic practices based on the physical presence of the poet (and/or
the poet's voice), and the theory that present-tense enacting of the poem
synthesizes communication into and as action. Among other things,
French sound poets such as Bernard Heidsieck, Henri Chopin and
François Dufrêne were reacting to the Mallarmean presence/absence
problem, that elegant complexity of the "*oeuvre pure*" which "cedes the ini-
tiative to words" as Mallarmé puts it, "to kindle up reciprocal reflections,"
and "profusions," and whose physicality was the special tenuousness cap-
tured through "touches of the finger" and "abrupt and lofty plays of
wings."

Sound poets sought to reground poetry by "bringing the work into
existence each time" it was enacted or performed, (see Heidsieck's

Partitions). "The hope and desire is to produce immediate, physical and corporal communication. . . Whatever the medium, this can only begin to be sensed in the amplitude of the moment of perception or particular reception" (Heidsieck, *Notes sur la pénétration*). Sound poetry produced and produces poetic forms oriented to performance in the fundamental sense of being presented/created/enacted for/before an audience.[4] Because of the immediacy of his language and the readiness of his creative capacity, Tarkos is at home in the world of improvisation and performance, and his work corroborates the kinds of action and reception aimed for in the sound poets' directness of communication. This immediacy makes for formal and thematic resemblances between Tarkos' composed and improvised work and, as the immediacy is fundamentally geared towards engagement, it joins for example Tarkos' recurrent endeavors to define poetry and his perpetual writing of manifestos.[5]

> . . . it's me who's inside
> Hail to you all the others born of fresh expenses
> for guarding any eatables for yourself and the
> cathedrals and highways and dulled deaf
> From fresh expenses, I form whatever to trap your eyes
> Even sick ("Monde de nés")

Tarkos' grounding of the poetic word also brings a Pongian thingness to the sound poets' presence, voice and aspirations:

> He opens the plastic bag,
> takes out one of the balloons, a blue one
> brings the mouthpiece of the flat blue windbag to his mouth,
> and keeping it tight between his lips and his thumb, and blows
> Pfff, Pfff, Pfff . . .
> ("Il ouvre le sachet en plastique")

Finally, there is the matter of the loop which could appear for the sound poets of the 1950s-70s as an effect of the mimetic fallacy/trope based on reel to reel recording devices, has its analogue in minimalist music such as Reich's, and has made its way back into contemporary French poetry via sampling and the latest technology.[6] Heidsieck described his *Derviches / Le*

Petit Robert as "a series of sound poems which having been recorded, should give the impression of turning back upon themselves, in space. Oscillating between circular contemplation of the navel and ecstatic levitation..." Traditionally, lyric poetry manages a synthesis of time and place, for instance in the shorter poems of Coleridge and Wordsworth. In Tarkos' work, returns are quick and constant, as we saw. Still a "contemplation of the navel" aspect is one of the many facts or grounds of the integrity of the writing:

> I'm swinging, it's the back and forth flow, it's automatic, its stupefying, it's palpable, it's automatic, it's stupid, it's palpable, don't let go, it's engaging, it's attentive. . . ("L'oscillateur")

as are returns to the subject of enunciation which are among the techniques that renew the poems' dynamism.

Also related to the performative is a dynamism that Tarkos shares with Olivier Cadiot and Valère Novarina (both of whom were vital by the mideighties). The intensity of voice, abundance of language and existential agitation of these writers are so great that performance in a more or less theatrical context at times becomes necessary to communicate the full extent of their work. The energy of the text for these writers is such that it "acts upon the actor."[7] Novarina, an *écrivain-metteur en scène*, explains the need for actors in the face of the perpetual and energetic language flow: "Actors must move quickly: writing always goes at full speed because language can only be understood in movement. Meaning only appears unexpectedly and off-kilter along the way." Both Cadiot and Novarina write for the page and for performance. Novarina seems to be especially important to Tarkos; e.g., "Space is inside of him. Space is inside of someone. A person is in space. Space is not inside of you. Space is not outside of anything. There is no longer anyone outside of space. You are inside of nothing... " (Prologue, "L'Animal du Temps" from Novarina's *Je suis*). The propulsive energy in these writers is so great that it invites breathed and plastic and temporal support. Novarina describes the process: "The text is fuel, energy. Something on paper that causes movement, that launches humanity into space in a new way, thrusts it and makes it fall anew."

In fact, Tarkos has a neo-modernist sensibility, driven by a powerful engine. His aesthetic is almost Steinian in its push, insistence and continuity of phrasing, and resembles Becket's in the evacuation of certain levels of referentiality and the hypertrophy of others. As some of the writing in this volume shows, Tarkos' range of references can be extensive. But he inevitably produces cubist-like turns, returns, cuts and perspectives that emerge and disappear from and through the representing medium. As in Becket, Novarina, and to some extent Cadiot, the writing process makes the movement of making a large part of its process, as a voice fills in the existential void. Where English-language readings tend toward the social and become almost exegetical acts of communication, Tarkos' performativity reveals the existential; his writing shows the casting of and giving life to and in language: how something that didn't quite exist before becomes.

3. Ma langue est poétique

In the interview in this present collection translated by Geneva Chao, "Two Born," Bertrand Verdier perceives an arbitrariness in Tarkos' writing, and he attempts to get Tarkos to admit an irony behind the work, at least based on awareness of post-modern preoccupations such as the exploitation of the notion of the arbitrariness of the sign. He also points out to Tarkos that he himself has claimed the Mallarmean, "You see, truth be told, it's the poem. . . the poem doesn't reveal the truth of the world, but it reveals the truth," and he notes Tarkos' claim "To tell the truth, uh-oh, that'll cause the revolution," referring to it as a technique for "dismissing a lot of contemporary writers." In the interview, Tarkos responds that his writing is not about showing [how] language functions. He contends that interesting writing, poetry, can only be "worddoh": procedures of distending, shaping, and making (functions and aspects and) words themselves stick, sticky and stretch. On the other hand, in *Ma langue est poétique*, Tarkos argues,

> The difference between hair and blond hair is slim, it tends
> towards a state of lack of differentiation of terms as they com-
> pose and because they compose there is dedifferentiation of
> the two terms of composition. The dissociation of conjoined
> factors is the general language process of poetry, *ma langue
> est poétique* on every level. . .

The juxtaposition of these two observations concerning stickiness and disjunction is interesting with regard to Tarkos' ambivalent comment concerning nominalism in the interview. From the realists and nominalists of the Middle Ages to contemporary moral and critical debates, beliefs in language's capacity to unambiguously state the nature of things have been opposed to assertions of its ability to indefinitely impose versions and modifications in the representation of things and ideas. Tarkos will not limit himself to one or the other discursive position. He believes in a real, even physical, power of words that nevertheless expects language to accrue efficacy or meaning through the variations that conceptualization, representation and reflection on the nature of language and poetry entail. Thus when Verdier attempts to discuss Tarkos' writing in terms of something like the now more or less classical Lacanian notion of *lalangue*, "the continuity of knowledge continuing without knowing it," Tarkos responds in the interview by calling language hormonal, physical and real, short-circuiting Verdier's reference to Chistian Prigent and Lacan by mentioning Fernand Raynaud, a popular comic of the fifties to the early seventies.

Barthes standardized and recapped Lacan's formulation, effectively clinching it as the expression of the Mallarmean aesthetic, and institutionalizing a post-structuralist nominalistic groove that asserts the inherent powers of (creative) conceptualization over mimetic doctrine (and the realist heritage and interpretation of Aristotle's: "Spoken words are the symbols of mental experience and written words are the symbols of spoken words. Just as all men have not the same writing, so all men have not the same speech sounds, but the mental experiences, which these directly symbolize, are the same for all, as also are those things of which our experiences are images" *On Interpretation*). For Barthes, "The subject him/herself is at the bottom of the work as an absence, every metaphor is a bottomless sign. It is this distance of the signified that the symbolic process [as writing] in its profusion designates."[8] While a work like Tarkos' "Les nuages" achieves a poetico-metaphysical rendition of existence, time, change and continuity, in Tarkos' practice, these dichotomies remain relevant and it is evident that in this work the Mallarmean and nominalist language constellating side of writing can never completely comprise, contain or co-opt the other "realist" side; presence and physicality are too entwined with the capturing and demonstration of the powers of language. Still, Tarkos writes so much that "contradictory" examples are easily found.

Christain Prigent wrote the introduction to Tarkos' first book, the collection *Morceaux choisis*, where he explains, "Tarkos' texts are multiple and abundant. One finds in him a true *puissance d'écriture, a copia*, as Latin writers put it. I am not going to enter into an analysis of this (it will come, it is inevitable)." Picking up that gauntlet for a moment we can note that older models and their imbrication of rhetorical, dialectical and ontological perspectives provide a useful means for understanding Tarkos' poetics and copiousness. Nominalist and realist approaches provide one way of considering the relation between thought and expression. Looking at the notion of *copia* provides another. In fact, Tarkos' copiousness is produced on all sorts of levels of language; more or less representationally, more or less metadiscursively, and comprised of different-sized word groups. In the fifteenth century Rudolf Agricola outlined several types of copiousness which can serve to describe Tarkos' work:

> Since by abundance and brevity of discourse, more than by
> any other means, we delight or offend [the first aims of
> rhetoric], and since moreover they are consistent with the art
> of invention, and it appears relevant to our purpose. . . [to
> explain that] fertility of speech arises either where we
> express few topics in many words; or where, although we say
> little about each and pile up many topics and stretch our
> speech not by size but with the sheer quality of things; or
> most copiously of all we say much about many things. (*De
> inventione dialectica*, trans. Cave).

Tarkos is a master at expressing few topics in many words; at saying a little about each and piling up many topics; at stretching his speech not by size but by quality of things; at saying much about many things.

While *Ma langue est poétique* combines several sorts of language, the following excerpts have been selected because they bear on some of the topics so far discussed. In these passages Tarkos' *langue* is his tongue and the French language, and his poetry merges with French poetry. Writing is not only a matter of word constellation or continuity, but breath. It refers not only to the paradoxes of Mallarmean or Bataillian aesthetics (Bataille: "silence is a word that is not a word and breath is an object that is not an object"), but to the physicality of language and the "magic" of expression. Tarkos' *langue poétique* rides the energy of language, generating words and

14

making them function objectively, subjectively, referentially and as "truth" in the movement of the production of the process:

> *Ma langue est poétique.* It is poetic in its unrolling and its pieces and in the wake of its pieces, it is not composed of words attached to words by accident, by suffering, by stapling corners and catch-lines and straps and frictions and stuck-together strings meticulously glued to each other to make up their length. It is not extended by a miracle in perpetual disequilibrium, it has breath, is a breath, is the breath, bypasses all obstacles in passing through the sublime effect, in continuing on when nothing helps it continue, with a last leap. Its breath pushes, reinvents itself in the heart of its breath, kissing the air. *Ma langue est poétique,* unrestrainedly, without stopping, without drying up. . .

> *Ma langue est poétique.* It is not a great gaping silence between the two columns of enunciation and their series of pure terms in compact masses that bear down in regular vertical series of facts and truths that set down, convene on the highest tracks pursuing an always heavier verticality further on, written with compactness, by truth, each more true than the other, more authentic than the other, coming from nothing, from a laborious effort of overpanic and undermining in the face of the prophets' continuing murmer.

> *Ma langue est poétique* in all its pores, in all its members, the length of its whole sublime sensibility revealed by its magic words, all its words, the least of its words is beautiful, pure, musical, fortunate, the words of *ma langue* are deliciously poetic. "Gnaw," one of those magical words. . .

4. The Composition of this Volume

The excerpts from "The Book of Squares of Earth" shows Tarkos' early incremental, concrete-like and sound constructions; his ever-present interrogation of the physical materials of poetry. An investigation of the possibility of grounding poetry joins demonstrations of its materiality, how

15

it produces, what it may produce; "explanations" of origin combine with putting the possibility of documentation in question. *The Train*'s movements through presence and absence involve a questioning of the subject position. Tarkos' tendencies to visual and sound compositions are active here in writing that resembles a kind of hybrid of the score of Kurt Schwitters' *Ur-Sonata* with a Becket-like progression. At the same time, like several of the works in this volume, it interrogates scale, impression and the loci where viewpoint and sensation accrue and come from.

In terms of the rhetorical/dialectical/ontological perspective discussed earlier, Process represents that aspect of Tarkos' work which shows what can be made of/with conceptualization systems and the ideal of descriptive inclusiveness. *Process* presents an encyclopedia of action. Settling longer and more categorically as encyclopedic entries/moments than the excerpts from *The Book of Squares of Earth*, it encompasses the close by and the far away, moving across history, anthropology, logic and sound. As language floats through ways of knowing or things to be known, the moving encyclopedia cracks the conundrum it presents: "He says the spirit of culture, agency construction after construction to add it to a series of constructions, exteriorized in a construction of structures increasingly extensive and complex and pushing degree by degree further while its spirit remains where it is and tries perpetually to understand always the same thing/ The panting panted together where the first to stop." Compatible with the lines from "hurt," "it paralyzed me but I'm just ahead, to the side. . ." and "it is rare and unusual for a feeling to be so interior that even the idea of asking it to go is absurd," the writing denotes levels of activity that pursue separations between universalizing statements, new constructs and individual experience.

"Words do not Exist" from *Sign* = plays out in two directions from the "realist" position. (1) It interrogates the suppositions and corollaries of conventional Saussurian theory to account for the nature of its object (and the possibility of writing poetry or anything else under such conceptualizations). (2) It seeks to take words. . . at their word, not as vehicles for concepts but the entities which move just as the nature of all things move. This movement, this process as Tarkos expresses it there, "attempts, it doesn't know." One of Tarkos' main motifs is the lexical field of the *boulangerie*, encompassing bread, "worddoh," dough, flour, etc. Here the amalgam of words as meaning fuses into malleable dough, and the material

16

end—words formed into dough as meaning— is what is worked rather than proceeding from concepts to words.

Flour's use of the space of the page, like the libretto "hurt," appears in extended verse-like form. It has a vast inclusiveness; encompassing by reaching for the palpable. Its material is the sensed, the felt, the detected, and what is put together and held together on different scales, including scales of production of various sorts. *Give* takes another approach. We are back again in movements within and with repetition, this time comprised of smaller verbal units, and with the invention and interrogation focused on a different syntactical and existential level than in earlier work: Rules of grammar are broken more regularly and subject and object pronouns, and positions, who is speaking, who is existing, how long who will last as what to whom become the matter (or dough).

Tarkos' *poésie proletaire* and a compositional technique resembling minimalist music are evident in *Toto*. "Language's energy must be tapped, wherever it may be: in dreams, in Mallarmé and on the back of trucks" Novarina asserted in the interview cited above. *Toto*, which dates from 1996-97, confirms this possibility. It does so by presenting language cells, similar to the rhythmic cells of minimalist composers or the wordless sound poems of Henri Chopin. Closer to Reich than to Glass, it presents movements within near repetitions and returns to cells that carry the "narration" through slow shifts. The excerpts from *Boxes* show similar phasing shifts, with a different compositional movement and a more diffuse narrative focus, while each box functions something like a traditional poem.

"hurt" deals with sensation and expression, playing with the distinction *in mente* and in *re*. Can the experience of pain be shared? Something akin to the minimalist composer's technique of overlapping is applied as much to language-as-content as to language-as-form. "Overlapping" in this case allows a variety of speakers to treat the same topic, and to explore a subjective condition, making the more or less traditional performance genre generally mimetic of the modernist project of construing dimension to the fragmented conditions of existence and social experience. —*Chet Wiener*

17

1) These writers are Tarkos, Oscarine Bosquet, Christophe Marchand-Kiss, Caroline Dubois, Cécile Gaudin and Albane Prouvost. This volume was never published.

2) Tarkos appertenance to the poésie prolétaire tendency is problematic. Jacques Sivan, one of the editors of the revue Java, considers the contradictory Mallarmean word-constellation and poésie-proletaire currents in Tarkos' writing to be its most controversial aspect. The next issue of Java promises a debate between Pennequin, Tholomé and Tarkos centered precisely on the question.

3) For poems in the form of circles see *Dix ronds*, Martigues: Les éditions Contre-Pied, 1999; "Ronds," *Action poétique* 142/143: 1996, 62-65; "Il fait flic," *Action poétique* 17: 1999, 175-181.

4) For Chopin this *before* was essential; he often repeated, "Poetry is action and precedes the action of crowds."

5) *R.R.*, a double A4-format poetry periodical Tarkos almost single-handedly put together for years, published at least one manifesto in each issue. Such items as "C'EST FAIT, LA POESIE EST DEFINIE" (". . . Definition says what is. Now Poetry exists. Now it is possible to love, to sell, to have poetry. . .") appeared next to "Le MANIFESTE du groupe 54," "Nous les pauvres" (which begins, "We the poor, we are poor. Poverty, poverty. We live, we, the poor, in poverty. . .")

6) See the works of Manuel Joseph, Anne-James Chaton, ...Éric Sucher and others. Also see the critical work of Jacques Donguy.

7) Novarina quotes are from "La combustion des mots et le sacrifice comique de l'acteur, entretien avec Valère Novarina," an interview with Bruno Trackels and Sabrina Weldman, *Mouvement* 10: 2000.

8) In English putting in "the" has the effect of making the truth seem to refer to the "real" or the realness of things and events, rather than to an abstract entity, Truth. In French, it could be read either way. Tarkos' comment comes as his response to the following questions "(1) Where are we poets today in relation to the notion of poetry, poetic form, the implications of poetry's existence? What has happened in the last few years that is really new, if anything? Are we witnessing the return to theory, its definitive rejection or a redistribution of questions and responses, etc? (2) Have avant-gardes, most notably between the two wars, supported totalitarianism in their work and their ideology? Does the notion of avant-garde necessarily imply totalitarian procedures?" The responses of twenty-five other poets also appeared in *Action poétique* 144: 1996.

8) "Classical criticism forms the naive belief that the subject is "full," and that the relation between the subject and language are those of content and expression.

The recourse to symbolic discourse seems to lead to an inverse belief: The subject is not an individual plenitude that one can remove or not from language (depending on literary "genre"), but rather an emptiness around which the writer weaves infinitely transformed words (inscribed within a chain of transformations) so that any writing that tells the truth indicates not the interior attributes of the subject, but the subject's absence" (Barthes, *Critique et vérité*).

9) See also, "I am a French poet. I work for France. I work in France. . . There is a link between me, the French poet and the French soldier. I am a soldier for France. The soldier of national defense protects French territory, French territory is the only place in the world where French is spoken. . . We should not be duped. The French poet that I am could only exist through the existence of the country that speaks French, whose existence is only sustained by the strength of its soldiers. . . I am a poet who saves his language by working his language, by making it work, by making it live, by making it move. . ." "La France," *Facial* 1: 1999, "une revue de merde," Ed. Charles Pennequin.

The Book of Squares of Earth (excerpts)

To go from Kilo/cm2 to Atmosphere, Multiply by 0.96784

I'm afraid. The tongue on the bottom. I can't not be afraid. Not be afraid, say but there are bottomless movements that glide on the surface. Tongue rakes land. Tongue covers a plot. Territory's a vast field. Territory isn't too big for the tongue, the plot grows and goes. Then tongue speaks, speaks, the possible combinations multiply, undo, unstitch, amplify, multiply, come and go, slow movement of verb moving on the surface, tongue rakes, land's dry, long time since it's rained, land's muddy, been raining too long. Land can't take in all the water that falls.

127 Words with one Vowel and Five Consonants
To go from are to acre, multiply by 0.02471

A work, what work under the conditions you put yourself. What working works. He's freed. From what hasn't yet, from a still-living mass, from this is that and that's how and here's how. Shivering. What rule. And courtesy, and politeness, and feasibility, and the location there that he to put himself. The architect's drawing where you want it that should be done said. He's crazy, he's free. The walls of that put itself and has to put itself put itself to twist the act. They don't want that it must happen.

67 Words with one Vowel and one Consonant

The plot shrinks. Yesterday, another letter ended. It'll be missed. Poverty continues. There's always one missing. It gets hard. One pack of words less. And a whole way of speaking and thinking this way less, I don't know exactly what'll be missing and the words already missing to say it, I can't say it anymore, I don't know what letter's the next to be missing. Poverty. The growth of the restriction of the thinning plot.

JOY JOY JOY JOY JOY JOY PLUMB JOY JOY COME FROM ON HIGH JOY JOY JOY
JOY JOY JOY JOY JOY JOY JOY JOY PLUMB JOY JOY COME FROM ON HIGH JOY
JOY JOY JOY JOY JOY JOY JOY JOY JOY JOY PLUMB JOY JOY COME FROM ON
HIGH JOY JOY JOY JOY JOY JOY JOY JOY JOY JOY PLUMB JOY JOY COME
FROM ON HIGH JOY JOY JOY JOY JOY

Restriction: a light movement of loss from feet to weight. Where
to put the feet. No longer bottomless. Put hands, put feet. Say
that not by this, not by what's that. That you can't. It's not
done this way, it's done this place to this place by walking.

Finite state automaton (l.m.) Finite state automaton Finite state automa-
ton is a set of nodes representing states and the arcs that link these
nodes

And then progressively, it is progressively, but there's no other
movement.

To go from acre to square foot multiply by 43650

      The plot is dangerously shrinking. The field and the
nutrients missing.

One Word with Two Consonants

Case: semantic cases are chests of drawers where each drawer contains
other drawers. Jew: Person descendant from the descendants of Abraham,
Semitic monotheistic people living in Palestine and remaining generally
faithful to the Jewish religion and traditions, inheritor of the sacred books
of the Hebrews. Descendant of Jews of old, descendant of Israel, person
belonging to the community, religion, people of Jews, descendant of
Hebrews, descendant of Abraham by Isaac son of Abraham, by Jacob, son
of Isaac, Jacob, who gave twelve sons to his wives and was after his match
with the angel named Israel, descended from his mother and father, is
where the vicissitudes and ancient history are in fact to be found.
Aborigine whose unknown name was given by the peripeties of a turtle
and an armadillo, the turtle was tired and rested under a big flat rock, an
armadillo came, saw the turtle, and said . . . etc., etc., etc., (a whole story)

A Z △ å E R T Y U I O P Q S D F G H J K L M W X C V B N a z e r t y u
i o p é ' è Á à ˘ , Ô ° Ó ¸ ; ? . ! : ú Ê q s d f g h j k l m w x c v b n Ù , -

or   75   letters   of   the
alphabet   for   7865445654
combinations.

Directed tree (l.m.) Arbre orienté
Simple tree having a summit R called root, such that it is not the origin of
any arc, and each of the other summits are the origin of one arc and one
arc only.

—Translated by Stacy Doris

The Train (excerpts)

the days plays
the days days
the days days gulp
the days days gaze grass
the daze days graze

Ta na ta na ta—ne te ne te ne te ne————————to no to no to no
to no——————————nor yr nor yr nor yr nor yr————————————
————————ah na ah na ah ra ya na yh ra yr——————————let me let
me let me let me let me let————————————me my me my
me my me my me my me ma————————————————no me
no me no me no me no me no me———————— my don't owe me—
————————————————my don't go way————————————
my can i ran the ran to can————————————of way tie i—
————————————i weight——————————i can icon w
want————————————————i'm out away————————————
————————————my lash i no——————————no lash i no——————
——no hoot i won't——————————no crash i won't——————i don't
crash up——————————twas not my slap——don't crash my mitt-
-don't crash so rash——————————no hush i no——————no hoot i do
————————————no slap i wrap——————————no crash oh lash——————want two

———————————————lull my nul——————————my is not
i no this nil ——————————ive got nought ————————define ought
mine——————————my hush no lull no nul——————————i not had
to hail ————————no hail i no ——————————far not i'm not my own
———————————————to hail my not so far——————————
——————————————i don't waylay, don't give my hoot, hoot not my
boot, not led my shoe, not hail my boot a hoot is moot, i'm
no, is so, won't go too slow nor rasp to grasp, to wind or
grind, i don't grind, i don't hail, i didn't say, i hail my flay—
——————————this marl, this won't me hail, this head's to fail——

_____

———————————————heads frail my ——————————not my
marl——————————i don't marr me——————————
————————i don't say, i said not nor had said not, nor did not nec
———————————————don't butt in——————————don't
now no——————————i don't know what's——————————its not-
———————————————the hat of it——————————
————————i nuke a do————————i to allude ——————————don't lewd
———————————————the me of this the twin of i won't nul
blast——————————the twin of weight ingrate ——————————
————————i dont care don't sweat sm stuff————don't crap my bluff-
———————————————————————i no i'm not this
not is, i thrash———————————————————————i cant
not——————————don't pop pulsate————i've i and me and ive
this and ive the end i'm the, and i say i not and multiply————
———————————————me, i, this the and i pop pulsate——————————
——————————————perambulate——————————
—————————————————————————————i crash
———————————————have i not twin————i's either————i see there—

————————pop pulsate————i have are not————i not
my miss————that i no had my miss————are you my miss
i hurt my wrist————————ambulance————————
————ambivalence————————amenity————————amphibian————
——i jump i not in it, i don't get up————————————i've probably
still water wet————i won't get up————————————i have no
wet, i have their water not had yet————————i there had not
——i there had not their pop————i don't want it so————
————————————————i start did not upon————————
————————————its the same————i won't get up————
————————a twin of what i did not start————the twin of what
i'm not to start ———————— the pop of what i's not of them-
————————i've none there————————i've none of what i
not————start then————————————————————
————————————————————————————i's not even
i get up————————————is taken not to even up, i am not
to jump to out, i've the same———————— ————————
————————————————————— —————————

————————————i'll not sell————————i'll not sell————i'll
not sell————i'll not sell————i'll not swell to sell, i
do not seek to sell myself, i'm not to sale, i do not swell, not
seek to sell————————————————————i do not sell
————————— —————————
————————— —————————
————————————————————————————
————————————— —————————
————————————————————i not my lie————
————————i never nay————————————i'm not i nor
them—— ————to sigh————its no————————

———————————— ——————————————————
——————— ————————————————i no is————————
——i no—————————————i not back off—————————i no
don't know how back off, he will not back off for now————
————————————————————————i do not go on————
i don't get up——————————i don't lean down, dont never
lean, to lean in vain—————————————————————

———— ——————————————————————————
— i set down there—i will not set my bet down there for no-
w————————————i don't infringe—————————i no is
ever there—————i no lean————————————i no
to wane——————————————————i vow to wow————
————————————i made of it myself a vow, my vow————
—————Hubbub——————————Here Wed——————
——i not and me——————————————————i this no this to
me————————————i this——————————————

——————— ——————————————————————————
————————————————————————————i, this mix
————————this won't grind up, this don't mow down, this not me
grind this grind no, this grinds me not, this mows me not,
this mow not, this not null—————————this never have to null—
——————————————————————this am not nor one nor i nor i
north, nor ice endive you all, nor dump for fun—————i them
there not me nude, nor not me hail, is not this want, this not
stand up————————————————————————————
————————————————————i no it mow————
————————————not is i not that which i is—————————i aint
but word, i aint me——————————————————i aint
too good to choose, i aint me, i me, i wing to be, if i is only-
i, toss and dive————————————look at me-it-he o'r there—

27

————————i's not no thing————————————
————i's me, i's i ————————— ————————
————————i say no ice, i say ice nay, i snay there's ice no , i
snay, ice in eye, i say ice may, ice naysay no, i say it's snow,
ice snow i's know, i know ice so, i slice that ice, i slice twice
ice, i say i no, i know————————————————
————i did not lie i know———————— i want it to
————————i see no more————————————i see
nomad, i no see knee————————————i deny no see————
————i want this to————————————i say————————
i don't fall in————————————i say ice————————
————————i's————————i's————————tis i————————
————i's not a fray————————it's i no way———— it's no———— no tis,
tis i, i tis ————————————————no ice————————
—— i's nice, i's not————————i's no say, i's no way no i no
not lie not slay not say————————————————i not is
got, i's not, not want to got, not want to get, ————————i no
is i no not is not ice————————————i no way get, i no
get into ice, i won't get me————————————————

————————————————————————————————————
i won't ice snay my————————i won't get ice, i twice my
ice, i don't entice————————————————————
i don't get mice in ice————————————————no mice
my————————i don't mice ice i's————————eh————————
————i don't ice mice————————i don't get mice a rice————————i no
get twice————————i am not twice————————it lies on lice————————
i don't get twice————————————know lice a rice————————
————————i know to not, i not tune oh————————not i, no this, not
i this not mitt————————i mitt a bit, not that, not this, not my

—Translated by Erin Mouré

28

Process (excerpts)

husband and wife, or two brothers or two
sisters, or mother and son, or a daughter
and her mother. Their two names remain,
Gobdelaa and Kasdoa.

> Remembering the reeds that enclosed the
> garden, or the little piece of ground behind
> the house. They were attached to the road
> fence. I turned round enormous holes dug
> very cleanly into the earth of the little piece
> of ground, I don't know why, on a small
> bicycle. I fell with the bicycle into the bot-
> tom of the hole. It was at the period of the
> third year of the reign of Pouki I who reigned
> after Ira when Pouki II reigned in his place.

In 747 the Chinese expedition under
the leadership of the Korean Kao
Sien-Che prevented the joining of the
Tibetan and Arab forces and took Gilgit
prisoner. The following year, the Korean
went and decapitated the Turkish king,
so the Qarlouq and the Arabs taking the
king's side subjected Kao Sien-Che to a
defeat at Talas and the region of Talas
passed into Wigur hands.

> An animal's Name is a good animal's
> name if it is written in purple typo-
> graphic ink before 1986 or, after 1986,
> in parma-violet hectographic ink or in
> mineographic ink, on paper.

There is no bush so small that it
gives no shade. And there is no
worm so small that it does not curl
up if walked upon and there is no
saint so small that he does not ask
for his candle.

> Lou pichot barquet fendié
> l'aigo sarié moun chale, ma
> coungousto, de lou vèire sèt
> an à mi pèd barbela.

The inside of the sex, the outside of the arms, the outside of
the sex, the skin of the limbs, the face of the being, the whole
of the story, the eyes or the modesty and the trembling or the
silence and the gaze or the hidden and mystery and grace
and beauty or the presence close by or far away of a living
form close by or far away of a feeling close by or far away of
a terror close by or far away of the harness tying by itself and
tightening close by or far away or the sweat or the tearing
close by or far away.

> Eradicates the strange curls of logic, of set
> theory, of the theory of numbers. The
> solution is the prohibition of forms of self-
> reference, separating the levels of expression
> and excluding valid structures of "void of
> meaning," this square, because they do not
> belong to language, nor to metalanguage,
> nor to meta-metalanguage, nor to any lan-
> guage.

> The dark between the
> stars is there, quite visi-
> ble. Good surface. That's
> looking far.

She came in, she took off her shoes and sat
beside him on the bed, and she kissed him, he
kissed her, her mouth on his mouth, his tongue
and his lips on her tongue and lips, her tongue
in his mouth, his hands slid over her, she lay

down, he took her in his arms, she lay beside
him, he slid his hands and enveloped her.

ILL [he] is for the French their soft conso-
nant rolling the l, ill has disappeared. Ill was
in soleil, sun, and bille, ball. Its softening was
like that of the Italian gli. Elle [she] disap-
peared at the end of the 19th century, and is
only found, threatened, in certain remote
mountain areas. Ill is replaced by yod, a semi-
consonant which places Ill on y.

The acrobat, the sailor, son of
father-in-law, carnies, the
sprinter, the hanged man, the
athlete, the gymnast, the
trapezist, the crucified, the
rapt.

Then the kingdom of Ani was annexed to the empire. Shutting up Kakig
the king of Armenia. But Seljuk of the tribe of the Oghuz, and the men
dedicated themselves to the service of the Ghaznevids, they went to con-
quer India, then installed themselves at the frontier of the Empire held by
the Spanish. And while the Arabs of Sicily were fighting with the Arabs of
Africa, and the Lombards of Capua were fighting the Lombards of Naples,
the Franconian Conrad sends the archbishop of Strasburg and the
Normans of Rainolf into Italy while John the Orphonotrophe sends into
Sicily 300 Norman knights and 300 Norwegian knights and the best of the
empire, they conquered the armies of Africa and Pandolf III of Capua at
Syracuse before the revolt of the Normans and during this time a Russian
troop attacks the empire and the Pechenegs sent against the Turks revolt
and install themselves in Bulgaria at the borders of the empire and the
emperor sent the best troops from Asia, while the Seljukids fight a
Georgian contingent and invade Vaspurakhan.

My tongue has only a few hours on the road ahead
of it. In the Iranian restaurant, the girls as beauti-
ful as Togo women. They hold their hands one
towards the other, palms one against the other,
place the right index finger under the left thumb,
and the right thumb against the left palm, snap

the right middle finger against the index finger of the left hand, finger-snapping, noisy rhythmic snapping, middle against index, the girls are dark-haired, they applaud with their fingertips. Not to make a noise.

> The transformation of mammalian reptiles into mammals was progressive and continuous, it is impossible to find a definition of mammals.

A fringe of signs, on the edge, before nothing, after, nothing. Get by with that. There will be a word like a fringe in the night. There results that the theory of confirmation consists of a definition that applies to cases that can not be described other than as cases to which it applies. Once more we obtain the result that anything confirms anything.

> There came a bear out of his bearhouse, came a fly out of his flyhouse.

Unbutton your jacket, unbutton your shirt. Grab violently and simultaneously with your left hand the lower left corner of your jacket and the end of the left sleeve of your jacket and grip. Slide this left hand and your whole arm following through the left sleevehole of your shirt, the left hole of the left sleeve being found placed on your left shoulder. Pull your shirt by lifting it from behind around your neck. Grab violently the end of the right sleeve of your jacket and at the same time the right lower corner of your jacket with your right hand. Pass this right hand and the whole arm with it into the hole in the left sleeve of your shirt placed on your left shoulder from the outside to the inside. Slide your right arm through the two sleeveholes of your shirt and pull your shirt downwards through the inside of the right sleeve of your jacket, your shirt comes out of your sleeve. Throw your shirt away. Button yourself back up.

> I automobilize myself, I automotivate myself, I autostimulate myself, I autoheat myself, I autoannounce myself, I autoguide myself, I

autoadvise myself, I autoform myself, I
autopush myself, I autodirect myself, I
autoorganize myself, I autocoagulate myself, I
autobelieve myself, I autoboot myself, I
autoplug myself, I autohammer myself, I
autoimmobilize myself.

Onion, Stump, Circus
Bouglione, Sunlights,
Hand, Woman, Man,
Glue, Soft, Cuckoo,
Good, Give, Give, Give,
Sun, *Byebye.*

Things have a meaning, are a sign, it's a sign : texts have
a meaning, are meaningful, it's a sign : fate and what's
left. It lies down in the clumped totality of little things
that gather and are after the fact, must be, the little
things that have written fate, it isn't done tomorrow. The
totality is the totality of what it contains, it lies down. Not
a sign is missing, not a detail that clashes, not a detail less,
not a fragment lost, lies down and lies down like that,
gives the totality with itself and lies it down, not a sign
that doesn't make sense in the end, that is not reasonably
a part of the whole that is already beginning finally to
make a true sense, that will be its sense. Zones.
Ah! Ah! Ah! Yele, oh Yele! The fire has roasted him,
great Ezuzum, the fire has killed him, great Ezuzum, the
fire has eaten him, great Ezuzum. Ah! Ah! Ah! Yele, Ho!
Yele, Ho! The fire has eaten him, kri kri kri, the one who
wanted to eat us! Where is his big knife, the water and
the pot. Ah! Ah! Ah! We will laugh. Thank you
Ngemanduma. We will laugh.

A cammarus is a fresh water shrimp A field-
fare is a 27 centimeter thrush. A littorine is
a mollusc known as the whelk. A terebel-
lum is a worm in the cracks of rocks. A dace
is a fish in Swiss lakes. An eristalis is a large
fly, with a black and yellow belly.

33

In 1644 the Iroquois-Huron war ended
with the retreat of the Hurons allied with
the French and the advance of the Iroquois
armed by the Dutch, allied with the English
beaten by the French, pushed back to the
west, pushing the Wataways to the west.

He was called Ngo, they were called Ngo, Ngo Han
and Hen, they were called Ngo Hao Hoa Hui Huy
Hun Hou Hue Hyen Heu Huong Hang Heng Tan
Tin Than Thin Thang Thi Tao Toa Tan Thanh Tak
Chicho Chung Ching Cong Thanh Cong Nghia
Sreng Cong Dinh Lang Dinh Tue Ew se Guech Ky
Baleng Bibog Song Sing Sieng Seang Phap Que
Phien Phuong Po Hun Sue Hout Sholy Son Long
Bour Seng Cheng Hak Babogog Bassoyog Elysee
Bapa Eleonor Babouloul Belep Hermine Biwang.

I woke up, up this mornin', cryin'
canned heat 'round my bed, run
here somebody, take this canned
heat blues, run here somebo and
take these canned heat blues
Cryin' mama, mama, mama, cryin'
canned heat.

Tour de France: the shoot. Arrese beats Bjorn Borg in the Monte Carlo
tournament, the dome of Saint Clair of Pompignan fell down on Saturday
night killing seven people, the government forces of Kabul have fired
three SCUD missiles, the London zoo feeds 8000 animals on the admis-
sions takings since 1950, but the number of admissions has gone from
2,000,000 to 1,000,000, in August of last year inflation was 1000% in
Bolivia, the sale of condoms and contraceptives is prohibited in Ireland,
the parliament of North Ossetia has declared a state of emergency in
Vladikavkaz after the confrontations between Ossetians and Ingushes, the
photos of fourteenth century jewels hidden in a sixteenth to seventeenth
century cauldron , which were found in nineteen-seventy-one, have been
sent back to the twenty-nine countries that were under the domination of
the Empire, twenty-one plays by Thomas Bernhard have been performed
this year, the compounds in which twenty appears have hyphens when they

are smaller than one hundred except twenty one, the series with eleven jump twenty ends with sixty-one, is written twenties when it is multiplied following a hundred or a thousand without being followed by an additional number, is pronounced van before a consonant unless the t is pronounced, is pronounced vant if the t is pronounced d, is pronounced vand in twenty-two, not vang, W has three brothers, the first kills himself at twenty-four, t pronounced and hyphen, the second at twenty one years of age, t pronounced interposed without hyphen, the third at thirty one years of age, thirty-two takes a hyphen, he says the spirit of culture, agency construction after construction to add it to the series of constructions, exteriorized in a construction of structures increasingly extensive and complex and pushing degree by degree further while its spirit remains where it is and tries perpetually to understand always the same thing.

> The panting panted together where the first to stop has lost aqittuq, haqalaqtuq, hiqnaqtuq, illuqumajar-nuarmatuq, immipijutuq, marmartuq, niaquinaq, quattepaartuq, quiarlittiaq, quanaqtuq, armerniaktok, niakorniar-tuk, qiarutsiaq, qiarvaktuq, uqsiqtuk, sirqusurtaqtuk, ullu, huangahaaq, aquittuq, iqusuttak, iurnaaq, siurnaq-tuq, pirkusiqtuk.

I had fallen into the hole turning about it,
where the sun hits hard and where the mis-
tral blows strong, the house was called l'es-
candiado as they said, the rays of the sun,
lou dardai di souleidoet follows by empu-
ravon dins l'er un lusent tremoulun kindled
in the air a bright trembling.

> Material things, at least, are made of natural parts, all entities that exist arise from small natural and simple parts, because what exists comes from pretty little natural and true and wild and sincere neither vegetable nor mineral nor animal nor human, seeds.

We went to buy some russets, some jonathans and

35

some lemon yellow goldens, she didn't want to look at the names, we left, I had met her ten years earlier, since then she had lived for ten years and you know what that means to live for ten years ever since. We went into a restaurant, a funny customer told her oh it's you we've known each for ten years and there you are, etc, had to say it.

She was in viscose in shaved velvet in combed jersey in rabbit skin in polyamide in angora in elasthane in tergal in wool, she was bound low-cut draped opened crossed fluid and supple, she was elasticated buttoned shouldered pulled over overstitched overstitched overstitched, she was fuschia violet coral peach emerald yellow ecru khaki sky with zipper closure and darts in the back.

She said everything can be bought, to explain why she didn't like poetry. We didn't walk in the streets, we drove from one Chinese store to another. It's the rainy season in Paris. I went home quickly. I asked myself again: do you know how to say there is a meaning because you can see clearly that there is a meaning. Squares squared between themselves.
We played just the two of us, it was Tuesday. All night long in the moonlight.

A slipping in the hand, leaving it alone, listening to the noise it makes, drifting, watching. The shadows weave, the rivers flow, fall, pull. Sitting down on the river.

Then a double night contravention, 450 francs for the non-functioning of the lighting apparatus of the rear license plate, apparatus in apparent good condition, then 450 francs for the crack in a piece of orange plastic on the cap of the front left indicator light in good working order, then the tire with ridges not deep enough, the erroneous address on the grey card, and the mirror of the right exterior side mirror, and crossing a white line. Then, police precinct, rue Lecourbe, Paris, 15th arrondissement, motor vehicle and paperwork control office, a single poster: the chipeau duck, the golden plover, the red nette, the scamp and the peewit may be traded until the 10th.

> The snare duck, the poker, the winter teal, the coot and other anatids until February 29th.

A is different to O. A and O must be pronounced. Show the incredible difference. Aaaaaaaaaaaaaaaaaaaaaaa / Oooooooooooooooooooo. Impregnate yourself with the pronunciation, pronouncing long in the mouth. Vocalizing a continuous a. Then a continuous o. Feel the evolution, the complex metamorphoses in the mouth. Keep the a, hold the a and slowly, gradually approach the other sound you know, delicately, the a is still there and think of the o, keep the sound a and try to reach through the sound a the sound of o by deforming the a as much as possible while keeping the a, the more it ap

Suddenly Orange becomes Lemon and Mint becomes Cumin, the molecules are inverted, right hand, left hand, the perfume metamorphosed.

And hup! A little acrobatic turn in the air, the loop-de-loop of the spiraling angel and then hup! Both feet on terra firma. And hup! What a beautiful brightness the sky has, and eyes can see, and hup! Impossible to see further than the end of your nose, and hup! A turn for nothing and two steps back and hup! The water is warm and the body is floating, arms and legs relaxed and hup! The picture of a face, an image shrinking, straining, wrinkling, and hup! Cold, the same cold. And hup, left twist of the side of the body, lowering of the nape, undulation of the spine and then, hup! Silence. The quarks are confined. The quarks can not get rid of themselves like that. They hold, they stick, enclose each other. The dolphin, the butterfly, the trout and hup! A jump with the feet together, high and low, yoyo.

> Then he turns, he makes waves. The accordion of the barbary organ and the great eight. A woman of circassian race dismantling herself into 32 pieces, the dog men andrian jeftichjew and fedor, a tanned hide split from

the occipital bone to the base of the breasts of Aissa, twenty years old, georgian, the most beautiful slave in the harem of the emperor of morocco, a hottentot venus aged 13 wife of a bushman chief brought by the elephant-killer, the skin of a zulu woman, the operation of the man with the fork, the man starved to death chained in a castle for 150 years, the formation of man and woman, the head of a spy from the russian-turkish war injected with a greek medicine, the last living aztecs from peru, the beautiful angelila tattooed with 300 pictures with frescos and emblems, 18 years old, with 4,000,000 needle pricks. One two three.

> One two three. Jumps backwards into
> the air, the head turns, the whole body
> turns around the head, with a clean leap
> of the hams, with a move of the head
> turns the entire body, jumps, turning,
> turning in the air, turning still, Clown
> Gayton, one turn, two turns, three
> turns, the nape, Clown Hobbes jumps,
> tries in turn, one, two, three, the nape,
> Clown Aymor leaps forward, one, two,
> two and a half, the forehead, the clown
> jumps, Clown Wise, one, two, two and a
> quarter, they turn, turn, Toner, Lacy,
> Muller, Richard, Decock, O'Brien, one,
> two, the nape, turn no more, Clown
> Stark tries again, one, two, two and a
> half, two and three quarters the nape,
> the jumping clown Billy bets with the
> jumping clown Lowlow, one turn, two
> turns, loses control of his body, three
> turns, does it just once, feet, alive.

He played the drum di be di be di be don and the trumpet fran fran fran and the flute tooralootootoo relootootoo and the mi fa so the farelarirette farelarirette and the mi fa so farelarirette liron fa the cymbal dran relan dan dan relan

dan and the accordion yon yon yon tira lee tee tee reli ti ti
and the mi fa so the farelarirette liron fa and the violin tor-
leo totio rela totio and the racket clack clack toora loora
loora loo and the lute tira lira lira la and the dulcimer vrest
vrest brest and the rattle taka tic tak tac and the fly zip zip
zipaso and his behind crock poof poof and the bottle glug
glug glug glug glug glug glug.

        The dictionary I have, or at least which is there, is an old
sepia colored dictionary without a cover and without
first pages which begins with acephaly and closes on pan-
theon; since it's missing the cover and the first pages,
probably also sepia, I can not give the manufacturing
firm, however it exists and lives with me as it served my
mother who left it to me unless I forgot to give it back to
her and so from generation to generation.

—Translated by Fiona Templeton

Sign=

signifier = signified

Words do not Exist

There are no words. Words mean nothing. Words have no meaning. There are no words because there is a meaning, meaning has emptied words of all signification, has emptied them completely, nothing remains to the words they're empty emptied sacks that have been emptied, meaning has taken all meaning, left nothing for words, empty shells, meaning debates by itself, doesn't need words, meaning wants everything, wants to take everything, has its go, is related to nothing, words are related to nothing, doesn't want to relate, wants to keep making sense, cost what may, crushes words while it debates, while it debates by itself, one can't take words for elements of meaning, for elements of meaningful tirades, there are no words. there is the pressure of meaning which clings to the pressure.

Words are unusable. Words are replaced by clouds, by cloths, by pressure, by the lengths of speaking, the bits of speaking, by expressions. Expressions, monologues, are pellets, water-pockets, water-bombs exploding. Meaning comes to explode, explodes at the head of monologue, it's a shot, a good shot, a good find, a good expression. It's apt. Like ideograms that give an idea in one shot, the group of expression is a group that gives a sketch, a sense that means something, a single word couldn't, there are no single words, words come en masse, they mix, they fuse, therefore the element of meaning is no longer the word it's the mass of fused words, the cup, the pellet, the monologue, the earthly mass, the glaucoma, the hump, the ideogram, the sketch. The mass of fused words is soft, pliable, supple, has the suppleness of expressions, of many words linked together, of strings, of garlands, of rolls of garbage bags, links of sausages, of balloons, of trucks' inner tubes.

A word that wants to make sense makes itself many to make a group of sensed words to make a pressure of many words linked at once, melted in the mass of words, in all the senses, they put themselves in every sense, they melt, they are melted, they regroup in an indistinct mass to push a little pressure of sense, they don't want to be alone, they wouldn't know what to do alone, they run in packs and the sense of words is given by the sense they want to give by so running, is given by the pressure for which they strive, they have no other goal than to melt into sense, to disappear completely under the movement of melting which has as impetus to go give sense, to make a pack, a packet of sense, in a single sticking, in one try, at once.

Lacks equilibrium, is not yet fixed, thought moves, and this is not only thought, clouds move, sun moves, hours pass, minutes pass, places change, waves stir, tides are in motion, blood is a tide, the mind is a tide of blood, is a tide of waves, sense doesn't work for once, doesn't work at once, will make several attempts is not sure, is not reassured to have to go through matter to, matter squared, matter fixed, to achieve a pirouette in the air, to succeed in turning, to bury in sand, to sow, to assemble all that happens, which happens quickly in one sole pressure, one sole matter, at once, in a trickle, which trickles already, with the pulp in your mouth, with the pulp serving as a mouth, with all its pulp, the sense of the pulp, how could it for once settle.

The uncertainty given to sense does what it can, it attempts, the sense is in the uncertainty of its steps, of its trotting, trot, it doesn't go, as clouds go, breath uselessly formedly crudely always being sure to be clouds that float in the air, it attempts, it doesn't know, it doesn't know what will come of it, it attempts, it lacks the measure of what is good, of what is clear, of what is comprehensible, it slips, it lets itself slip, the word explosion doesn't explode, doesn't make the least noise, doesn't explode as it would like, has no accent, has no strength, it aims I mean, it aims to the side, it aims in the emptiness and passes into emptiness at full tilt, to lose itself, for nothing.

The list of words to be fused gives a soft dough. From which, the sense that everything you say has a dough-sense, has a dough of sense. Takes the form of a dough. Afterwards, the dough can present itself in any sense, reverse, turn, bend, twist, it always has a sense, it does not deform, since it is dough it can take any form it has no more or less sense full of sense of what you say, you can use and reuse it, stretch it out as it is elastic it doesn't break and it holds to the end of any manner in which it's pulled and contorted, it goes, it goes on toward the end.—*Translated by Geneva Chao*

41

Flour

pleasure will not be caught that way
it doesn't matter, that, flour

even a big spud disappears all of a sudden sprouting

polenta-cellophing
this is adoration

On the circumstance of people without hands

We devote ourselves
We struggle

you hear a closed place

it's not my eyes that see, my eyes don't see anything, it's me who sees

A
Don't you have the feeling of taking something from him, breathing,
owing?
B
The nicest thing is having thought about sandwiches and the café before
going
to work
going to the workplace

blooming

to color for what is really friendly

balancing is one thing

the greatest thinker is poincaré

that will occur harmlessly layers of swallowed matter
what can happen to me can only happen to me

trip: knife, spoon, nail clipper

so cold, outside

between M and I
the distance there is, that's for sure, between M and I

another baring possible by the clouds falling
the cone
to retail

attention (sirens) alert, imminent danger

a con a concrete a coffer coherent con almost completely full

to love: flat
(you) love: check
(I) will love: bowl
etc.

to travel world

Toto is not what he's not, is not false,
a biway/a highway/

I scare/I puff/the gong skin
Him jumps, Me, I don't jump

story of little pebbles and flights of stairs

little word on the ground what is she supposed to do
I don't: I don't tidy, I don't grow up, I don't filter: I have no antennas
lasting memory: sabard and the basket, benkaffouf and the rose, and the
kindergarten cut-outs
and the people without hands

1st day of heating at the edge of the woods
2 Blvd. Mrs. Mother 76 m. oasis cartwrights main fl.
hats and accessories
china winter white
jean terrien manager of goods
shops and market
the forest source of life
meter parking services
arcades and shop grillwork
little blue wooden sign white letters on the grillwork
office of CIVIL STATE HYgiene (under hygiene desk)
further on, hunting license

the surface of the sea was sensitive to everything said

arta paasilinna the hare

aio lax agor
a's guf

title of a cineto-syntax digest

the further past

notes the scent of the fig tree at the bend; the plane that goes by, the
        baraault station

the telling of what you'll want

taking the missing phrases from the breath, phrases
are missing from breath

an embryonic thing is a sort of embryonic thing

citations of law in a delay

on the manner of the manner at the field's very end, in great swipes of
pruning hook, harvest
law; solos, toasts, public storytellers,

from the sun rises to the sun rises
other phrases for the breath

the head bag big project of shadow and its girth; like a garbage bag

time is for discovery
flight detonated
everything goes goes everything

the number of family
dust-buster
side-bar on the back of the chocolate box
where so many are empty, the lungs are empty,
some words from the breath signed X

five minutes

which way does he go to get to winter
you're into the game that's for sure

you choose it yourself your way of thinking
it's outside the mouth, it's inside the mouth, it's eating

you have the list of the description of the prairie with the name of all
　　the plants

tongue, you are not very good at description
the show: I am very happening
From one-thirty to around two

you just need to not take it off
carrier is an adventurer

paul van ostaijen 1898 1928

merz mecano de stijl sturm the serious bloody last letting go
the only freie strasse
maybug; Dd 04 H2 the hard-boiled egg, the fan, dice
teapot from hell roach; evening of stock market of agricultural products
the stroking the belly

realism and the link to print the link the air

the fact of being mid-thigh in sense

(the new novel: I am not a child, I am hanging peacefully on an urban
tree smoking a cigarette)

146 holes in the sieve

there is a text of numbers

once things take shape like a head or something like that you have the
onion festival or the garlic festival, the grouper festival, it's the festival
day of, it begins and it's always suddenly a little hill of that, you got your
festival you got your head

I connect the hood with the brush broom, you see how easy it is:
there's really nothing to worry about

between the moment when the piston rises and the moment when the
    piston falls

the short hairs of life

the basin or the self and its the outline
the ground water, the cats

from the vehicle signaling on the place de la Bastille

a precise description of children's toys
you have lost the handles from the rackets, cup of the fun world

gas leak from the circuit scan of the exchanges of the umbilical mate of the
no step shot
kills

store: you want any kind of thing?

that girl's white skin

triangulation method

can sack-cloth be a mother?
I am the dental apparatus you had little
whose cover was marked F. Nietzsch
see the tire's round

the trampoline
analysis of a unexisten thing: tv for example

what which undertaking
that is, that the Factory comes to me

france sunday nathalie and johnny

there are several forms of forms of that which fade

riding
knowing how to choose one's food well and drink lots

to get to st petersburg
it's the first time I'm being asked that it will have to

the triage gets checked

the vomit of the girl in the family

rose vendors have the right to come inside, and not the clowns, what a
mess, on top of which I paid for my drink, you are really assholes

of course I miss her

surrealism: the smell of morning

bedee
bedeedee
missfire-fire
bee
dee

dry clacking ringing brief round heavy smoothing

I've got my grandmother's asshole

simple: there's a rotor

the one who makes the one who loves his mother

by clearing or cleaning

that thing, it's fine, I like it fine

the arms, I'm building up, I'm building up by kicking my feet

the sky is falling slowly. A dog breathes with its tongue

description of the package

could you get it off me, would you be capable please of
getting it off me from there,
I don't like it sticking to me

I bend to that, a dozen times then a dozen times several
thousand times then
I flake

it can take pleats, one can to make, one can take differ
example one one one
can bend like this to this to from to from to from to from

a hair is what is real. The only reality still really possible for sustaining
it. That single consistency can not let us believe that we are going to be
able to get heavier thanks to her but she sustains us and holds us, holds us
to believing that alone the hair still holds, in its mix of unpleasantness
and agreeability, the hair is according to circumstance soft or out of place
and ugly a single hair can become discouraging when a well combed tuft of
soft hair lifts and sustains by its number important and difficult to count
methodically the support of reality's hairs

then he will touch the weight

an onion would be obvious.

one is not going to leave on the sides

come cut fingers
hello grand substance

revolutionary song, I am happy to go to the factory

the holes can be very small

the brain rests it in its milieu
to what I have been sustained?

let a long brown horse

bron, I live in bron
and you are kidding yourself

auto eat anode
one has a thing
one has another thing

the form of chance

it happens it's lovely
a man in a barrel, is there a man in a barrel?

it isn't fear, it's the texturial function that worked
papered by the impulsive mechanic of substance brought for that

flips itself over like a flapjack
flipped itself over like a flapjack—what fun

on the greater number of drops outside field

the necklace of pearls or of faraway pearls
a necklace not of pearls, of other faraway things,
a necklace further and further away

the building isn't the noise

I must have forgotten to contact the contact, I did not contact the contact

you have already seen a clew cross a string?

the machine
835
327
6 10 0
infinitely memorizing eating screaming the days with screams

something nervous and brief like a tap of a teaspoon

have a heart clear of it

mouth open wide A bee
faucet, snail, apartment, aphid, gall, silver, tickle tickle
the limbs of chickens of cups

the positions come out clear then they are orientable
from the simple fact of their position

with the breast humming or purring
there are holes
when you sit that broadens there is a broadening of the world

or a hedge of poplars or a line of buses at the depot

the history of the faculty of thinking of the roundness of the skull turning

the weakness of the eye one feels it has no bones in this place

the hollow which stores space for combining for the pleasure of where the
series of the sacs

the partitions, they feed
a man noble handsome proud courageous arrogant my desire with his
frantic idea of you

aua acua aive wawa ewe aigue aguea
you have to automatize yourself

your own identity, your accession to your autonomy, limited reciprocity
where one who takes gives as much as he takes
a durability of what you are in his presence or not

it isn't because my mother is old and has a long coat of long
fur that my thought tatamizes
I do not look like a dog

I am too all me head down but like this I can do less
brow

the deregulation of air transports
I don't have fourteen arms

I get concerned

you will respect the general ambiance

the proper leaves a pegassy layer

one is not going to take a word but everything they have in common

I picked up a book in the ditch: it's a phone book

I let my hands slip into the gear of the fabrication of
hands, and go ahead avanti

I also think of something else, because I pay attention, I'm not crazy,
you never know

I forgot the ants
how a plumb line works with the square
I put it in the notebook to loved
survival helped by half
it smells; it pelts

it's strange getting eaten
getting eaten by whom?
by the eskimo family

the idea of getting eaten isn't dying

my tablecloth grows dim

international rights of insurance
in a sense one is photogenic

they follow each other thanks to the idea of following
a long enough necessary enough
worddoh and no method in followism

why don't weeks have names

say a dinner
or a very young girl seized by a spasmophilic attack
or a plastic bag
or the contents of a plastic bag

the presence of the night, we'll see tomorrow

to see the exit colors of the big ears

the head does not exceed the limit of the pellet

plumpage shapage touchage feelage

the soft-the-hollow round the angle-relief straight line drawn
the superstition that would signify something

where you see the layers of idiocy in order to ram full

toot toot the horn of the handlebar the piston the sliders the trombone
flute trumpet

there are a number of shoe sizes
oops the ball almost went on the pavement
dead drunk that means he is falling asleep, to fall asleep, that he has
fallen asleep, he's sleeping

a one time
forgotten
in a one time

to become a little animal all fresh

three is a name one remembers I know the names by heart by lateral
infiltration

"I just want to manage"

facts: fairies

—Translated by Norma Cole

Give (excerpts)

taken there the asked, so that your warmth wouldn't give
pleasure with gave being this my lost, you now
will say going is it once met this wanting
this wish, will be your desire choose the agreement, the coming the
always him and all this i you who this my will give me
why for we encountering and passing you
you do want a what's left that you like, to be attached know a
and you will take not given, and the accepting, me a
sees me let him give my had been given, fate always seen
mine you remember it give me to lose, for a
new one that in in the you to lose i we are to you
would say the good if you want some, why would i lose the way
know with keeping me not me even no wouldn't say you the right there
me, not the need for i was the know day, shut up me
do you believe me for you know the most you were

would he suddenly be was becoming this not given day's
the i that they alone would you say true to say the was
i how it has that's suddenly i'll accept it
you are it to me, you me attached truth, you to give my name,
would remain even me of the been was going gave you, i want some
for me this it and this had been seen i still there given always
i don't take, i to know still yours
would leave would be disown, i want for him of my if you in you
had the desire he given for the we know to give but you
that now but you with us our habits
we little sense that passed kept me chooses
that he yes i didn't give any another now it's i
give as i accept it is would give i you for taking
take you i he you have me the pleasure the need, will really have it
disappearing to have nothing, and the best is to give

if he is living, i wanting is not your way i was
would give i is your day, you-remember some go
i meanwhile you lost you will recognize, would lose more
had loves in me, you the doing i would have it from me
my heart, heart we know if i want me, where your agreement
your smell, the i-don't-know-why i continue

would want to give my give i no with this never
wanting i don't have why pain after having seen it,
incomprehensible a blow i'm living, more give me
need, there, from i passing becoming the little pleasure
the not for living, a of lost you i go to give some this
that was known, and with this agreement with you for i not and it's
to you mark you i love take her don't leave don't give
this way if you are in a moment, and am there, i will accept the that
why he's not the one who desires you it to give me

gives me an i forget, to say i my taking took with us
a why he me near the day it's i lost the by
that would do it, are you to you given would take him will take
her for me not quick enough, you're like that, the what is given
that i give this fact why that me again why
gives me life had none but what you are i me to go by the
at all, more and more, i have you it's i accept it go
is only a smell i keep quiet but with me
he takes me better, but with me, see he is more
incomprehensible, will say, will say me understood me
i everything always have you not one to raise me up
for this that that i asked for, if we know to whom to give

i have know, this you give me, i have in me what was me
not to you i you which more so, in a moment, in need go me
to give the making of that little that alone you are the little which my

accept give you from the little of my he i her me, for is you
why her would say pass by, the way of he it mees
you to give why i stay give if you will not say that
i always had it, attached the will you want this with i, i you he your
way your accept, i is it given him me the go and goes by the
i need, need you, isn't i will lose i forget me
is really me, if i want becoming see
in the sense of giving, at will to retract, me who have it
i give and will beget you, for taken sight, the urge to give
one day, i have it you lost it to give we will take it away from you
isn't i was like that i know why i lost i which i had
want i am living you will have it give to me again
from you i love the truth i warmth for the need
attached never to chose you took it for your life to live
you have it by i habit me giving always

i don't stay, me would leave me give you after lost
the day when it got lost with it was given i thought that you
why as soon as i we i lost, by my watching,
leave behind, keep know life that the day i put it up for watching
do you want to attach to give to mark to give your accept
sight, being, you don't know what became of love
one has gone by, intense, give desire lives, i who expects myself
i have it for kept will remain what that's i at all always
whose would it be so if you don't accept it if my happiness with me
accept it taking my you remember my newness
see my heart me past you are still there, you would come
accept it ever there, you i to you gave it it's a passing
i know the pleasure, taking your stopping for now, choose you
yours, why suddenly my stopping loses
this i'll accept for why to give the no i were one

smell is my given of passing by by you give it me
as me you'll take my heart i would give how
desire for you is the me i you knew the that there is always the
i so as not to accept it, i don't know why
now is past even suddenly to say
what had the who lost who it had met
want give pleases, more with me to give than it true for you
who takes it losing that's where i'm going where it would make
where i will have it after the fact in my we passing by
will be in my we was the he would recognize in you'll
remember, it will be you that we are
i have it the accepting, take my gifts why the pleasure
had a now the want was me it i take
a little should it disappear was in us which the new
you wouldn't want some quick i know that he wants, a smell, you

to give to take would i give meeting us which will say the
not true desire which had been the same need always with
this would want there the newness, one close to he won't say anything, i
have it in desire you are incomprehensible you know i love the need
is with the same and was the past denied, i accept i-don't-
know-why the being at all, i why the was

the new to lose the need, is with will recognize, is i gave
some not to say any more, will say to me lost, you
will one day meet should you disappear to make you disappear
suddenly feel my heart, my smell, never more
that smell, was that me, me attached, you remember
you but more i want it and more you are taken for there, is we
at once is seen passing now is the past
would be living why you give me it, i don't know
would it be my pleasure i send it to you, i give it to you

he would disappear, would want with who to give it, sign
my we encountering our meeting you keeping a mark
made, makes him disappear, makes him living, knows, makes him
disappear, he lives, he knows, he takes pleasure still given
so giving taking life, that ises me the giving it
after having the i would take remaining my becoming, i am going
to give to desire the that i will give you you will say that my
heart is this transitory make it right now go with an i you
you gives i suddenly the passage you will take
you will give if what you want became you i have it want you stay you
givens give the you that for regularly i say lost
i say why i lean a bit, a day it will make you

61

me you past the way of being i this to lose, me was given
and taken, take you from lost since give that it why
of my life, i have there, he day i asked the need that i have that he

has of giving, that keeping would disappear without taking the not step
not me the would you want nothing would have me taken me him,
    nothing alone
you take i forget i some wouldn't accept that you granting
even if i am still living i am all your warmth i was
why who me, you accept, namely me the little
strengthened i give the heart was always for giving yours
not this had been given the pleasure, is wanting to accept it
i saw it, now, you a first step not past in past
in truth, i you want for the lost you, lose the first
promise to live the little of you has chosen you he will lose your
will give that's coming will be that he from you will take life the i for
how i take want i choose i he where it to give
with you so would say are we in its trust
if it passed in its desire if it came in its passing
the i never had any but an i will accept it

i was asking him now i would have it i me want
if you could forget you were thinking it to me will he want it given
the which i take will he want to say i had i am i thought
i wanted, i you i would have given i give is you you
i me passing we you gave it he understood he says give
you know i am so he'd have given the is me is you
i gave it i, did i say give give you say yes
i give you you is it here me, alone i we know have it for taking
i you he for giving given knows you no when the it i
which seen me yes the it i me you me i given you, he it have true
give you you you given the you you passed you knows to isn't
is yes can to the it i you i alone wants me suddenly
from the your other yes has it alone lost quick that gives
know i is given you has you it has not i, he is you you
the me i he to have you it or i have that it, you i gave you give who

of you in person wanted was wanting give given where you me
i had it you to give i no one seen heard he give
he not i for meant the you gives i i me
i like when the to i have it have it heart the when taken, the
you you give he the i have to the been that passed to

—*Translated by Chet Wiener*

Toto

Toto redirects the head of the truck. The head of the truck squeaks and bounces back when he turns his head. The head turns well around the truck. Truck knows how to turn the head of his truck well. Truck parks, if he parks it's because he's not sleeping. Toto is going out, he no longer wants to be that which endures that. Toto is going out because the restaurant is open. In front of the door Toto sees straight. The world is straight. Toto doesn't stand out, doesn't turn his head from right to left the way truck does with the head of his truck. In his way Toto doses the breathed, breathing it is a trick. Toto has the trick. Toto turns up at just the right moment and hears nothing. Pictured sad to leave the restaurant as he exits because he's leaving. He buys the same bottle of oil again and walks with his bottle in the direction of his truck. There, he's sad to leave the sector. The truck's balls distance him from the one small aim he'd set and bring him back to the white cheeks. Toto doesn't set the slightest aim since getting to the truck's balls. As long as he has his pants down the balls and the cheeks of the truck make up for all that he'd put into the zone of his thoughts. His mind was set, his mind is set. Toto is not going to turn every which way. Toto is totally unconscious. He eats and pipes up. Eats everything there is in the restaurant and goes back outside. Looking right at the exit door looking right in front of him. He pans. The road out of the rest area is the one that is there. The other road goes around. And yet another one is the road in. Toto is not going in, he will leave the right way. Toto has a marriage. And has a mayoralty. Toto has three highways meeting at the same point. For two for three Toto has always perfected everything. Perfected. What abundant abundance. Around the point p, Toto has perfected. Toto who is marrying. Toto marries. Has encountered three highways. Toto at customs. Two customs agents on bikes. Has encountered truck. Truck is truck driver. Toto has honored the dose. Toto gives the dose. Has returned honor. Weds the dose. Toto perfected the doser of the dosage of the dose and of the dosed dose. Toto doses. Toto has perfected knowing how to dose that the dose has perfected the dose. Meets three customs agents on the highway. Toto doesn't go so far as not knowing how to dose. Toto makes it a point of honor to give a final point on the dose, to the knowledge of the dose, to the definition of the dose, to dose. Toto gives the dose its right measure. Toto measures the rightness of knowing the given. Toto gives? Of the customs says give. Toto reperfects adjusts to the current taste for giving to the customs giving. The other highway crosses. Toto crosses the other highway. Three highways cross. Toto is at point p when three highways cross in the same place. Three customs agents go across the bridge. When Toto goes by the highway three customs agents go over the bridge. Toto has perfected a passport to a bridge. Where? To a bridge. Toto puts all the passports back. Three highways promise. To find. Toto finding. Like three highways that promise, one that finds, one found, one finds. Toto takes the highway. Not the highway bridge, the highway he finds. One point in each saddlebag. Toto has a saddlebag. Toto has perfected taking the highway. One for all. Not for example one for all for once. Amidst for all for taking a direction, Toto takes for true. Toto bearer. Toto buyer. Takes everything for true. Toto bears truck's pants. Truck says get a hard-on at the idea of Toto without pants. Truck doesn't get a hard-on. Toto must bear truck's pants to his truck. Where is truck truck is at his truck. Toto doesn't bear his pants, Toto wears pants. Toto waits. Toto as all else is perfectly on time. Toto has perfected good night. So that even truck is on time. So that truck can also be perfect at night. Truck is not at his truck. Toto waits for forgiveness. Forgiveness doesn't come, Toto takes back his pants. Toto sets off again on the highway his pants under his arm to put his pants back on. Toto totally naked. Toto has spoiled his pants. Truck is in the middle of the grass. Three customs agents. Two customs agents go over the bridge. In the rest area truck pisses behind the fence. From the other side of the fence. Crosses the fence in the grass. Truck is on the other side of the area. Toto is at the end of the area. Toto gets a hard-on. Not seeing that he has a hard-on Toto watches asks forgiveness, forgiveness doesn't notice. Toto doesn't notice. Three customs agents go over the highway bridge when goes under the highway bridge to meet Toto. Toto going limp without noticing looks at the truck's open door. No customs, no truck. A chaffinch whistles in the rest area. Toto who notices nothing asks. Truck pissing on the fence at the end of the area. Toto looks the other way toward the other part of another end of area. Toto has perfected going limp without noticing. Toto doesn't notice. Toto grabs his tool to piss. Toto gets a hard-on. Toto holds his stiffening tool in his hand and can't do anything with it, he doesn't do anything with it so he waits. Toto waits. Toto takes good measure. Toto asks robot to take him in his truck, robot asks him to wait, Toto waits. Robot has a drink with anode. Two beers and two empty beers. Probably car's and bank's beers. Bank goes home in his automobile. Truck who says get a hard-on says see Toto get a hard-on. Toto doesn't notice. Truck passes the highway bridge. Car passes over the highway bridge. Toto goes by point p and puts all the other passing points around. All the points pass around. At one point on a point of one of the three highways that cross. A portion of the highway. The chaffinch whistling on the rest area thinks Toto's an idiot. Toto's not an idiot doesn't see any chaffinch. Toto sees truck piss. Truck has the back of his pants but not the front of his pants. Toto asks truck truck why are you pissing. Toto asks forgiveness, forgiveness why are you passing. Toto infers everything. Everything is just on time, even truck is. Truck pisses. The fence holds. The grass. Well dosed Toto giving the definition of the dose. Toto has a marriage, Toto marries the dose. Truck has his back turned. Toto infers under the bridge. Toto infers on the bridge. Let's color. Toto has perfected two doses, Toto says to give still more than two doses. Two doses still aren't enough. Two saddlebagged customs agents go over the highway bridge. Car crosses the carbridge. The highway produces even more than two trucks. Toto wears pants. Truck wears bigger pants. Truck with a hard-on wears bigger pants. Truck takes the highway, the biggest. Has taken. Says sees Toto. Toto says doesn't see truck. More than once idiot goes under the bridge. Forgiveness doesn't even notice Toto. Toto inventor of the dose. Toto invents the dose. Toto inventing the dosage. Toto from behind. Toto lowers his pants. Truck lowering his pants. During three highways. Toto and truck, truck and Toto. Takes distance a great distance. Takes two great distances. Robot takes two of the boss's beers. Boss gives two to robot and two to car. Car and robot at the boss's place. The point is out of true. Pants' stitch-points are out of true. The point of pants' stitch-points are out to be taken for true. Toto sees true. Toto takes for true. Toto sees for true. Sees the length at arm's length, Toto sees the dose, from all of his height. Toto has three lines. Toto is given gives nothing. Turns his three lines. Shoots his turn. Toto is not a very long trip. Toto does not want to be the whole length of the trip. Toto is stopped. Toto is a very short line. He thinks with the whole length of his arms. Toto has two lines. Toto thinks all of the length of his entire height from feet to head. It's the same length, Toto sees only one length from all his height at arm's length. Toto sees two identical segments. Toto sees no further than the end of his two arms, Toto is a very short trip. Toto is stopped. Doses true. Toto believes everything he sees. Toto has distance at arm's length. Truck distances Toto. Truck takes some fake dose. Truck says in truth Toto looks out of true in the distance like a chaffinch. Toto takes it. Forgiveness passes. A customs agent whistles. A bridge straddles. Truck has a meal. Toto waits. Sambon takes the night. Toto waits for day. Anode is already drinking, car isn't late. Car changes place with anode, car gets on top of anode, car eats anode. The night perfected. Toto takes the night for a fee. The night takes Toto for an idiot. The truck brakes. An idiot passes for a night. Toto perfects a passage. Truck where the fence pissed. Three fenced highways. The bridge which weighs. Toto perfects a passage in the fence at the point where no one knows where anymore. Toto invented a passage point. The truck brakes and reaccelerates but anode doesn't watch it. Robot plays. Everyone eats and drinks more than those in the toilets. Toto perfects a passage for a foot through the fence. Wherever. Toto perfects a point where whoever can pass a foot. Robot drinks. Bank at the pump. Robot and bank at the pump. Truck parks. It brakes and reaccelerates. Truck's head squeaks when truck reaccelerates. Toto at the bar counter waiting having waited for truck or pictured. For truck or pictured to pull up to the station. Bank enters. Bank takes a seat at the bar at the table. Everyone plays. Fun. Toto meets robot at the boss's bar in the gas station. Toto takes what, Toto takes the highway. Robot enters the restaurant, eats everything there and goes out again. Goes out again again. Borot eats to the brim in the restaurant. The restaurant is open. Roll watches a heavily made-up and well dressed woman come in to pay for the gas. Boss has seen everything. Roll is a family and has one window. Who is sleeping in the truck? Truck puts his glass on the flat of the table. He has several dirty beer glasses. Rotor asks roll if he's his friend. He is looking for a friend of his own. Rotor scammed him, Rotor scams everyone. In playing and in not playing. Rotor says it's not me who killed killed. Toto knows how to test. Toto knows how to dose his tester. Toto is the happy medium of dosing in his sector. Toto has 5 segments, Toto goes straight. Wherever Toto goes, Toto goes straight. Roll has given rotor a big slap. Toto didn't see anything, Toto has his back turned. He doesn't know what's in his back, he has never tried to find out what was brewing in his back. Toto's back brews. Just seeing Toto is enough to see that he is a doser, watch him and you are better dosed, just by watching him. It's contagious. He's a beer drinker. Truck is, Pictured is, Tourniquet is, Robot is. Meanwhile everyone talks. In the meantime Toto doses. Toto lasts as long as his dosage lasts. Toto lasts indefinitely in the sky. The forces and the methods are the same. Tourniquet smiles, is smiling. He smiles for tray, cupboard, to place opposite, cement, take a glass and a fork. Tourniquet smiles daily. We are about to see Toto go out. Toto knows what he's doing. Toto knows how to produce a possibility when he adjusts a good dose. He is always within the possible with method. He has everyone arm in arm. He asks pictured frankly to see him leave with him, he would love to see them leave together. Boss chips in and rearranges everything. Everyone has eaten to the brim. Boss just has to clean everything. Car eats anode again. Pictured says he's pissing again, pictured says he's turning his back. Truck has a white ass. Everyone is just about under the table. All fall at once. Toto falls in at just the right moment. Toto knows how to dose. Toto on vacation. Toto near the place of his training. Toto straight as an i. Is on the rest area that makes the sound of the long trajectories always passing in the same direction at the same place. Is all there is. What's there? There's Toto who is on the area. And friend who's killed. Only a friend kills a friend. Pictured Bank will go back to pay for the gas taken from the pump. Robot stays at the pump. Will go back to pay for the gas taken from the pump in the restaurant. Toto asks how much, Bank asks for something to drink, Truck asks Forgiveness. Pictured asks how much. Boss tells truck he didn't see forgiveness this night. This night is dosed right. Toto asks for how many nights. Let's color. Let's approach. Toto approaches truck for the first time in his life. The boss approaches Toto. Truck approaches pictured. Pictured approaches bank. Robot, Bank, Pictured and Anode have fun. Toto doesn't answer boss, Toto is sure he'll pull it off. It sure is Toto. Toto looks in the air to see the dosing stunt fall. Toto breathes at every stunt. He knows how to dose the stunt of drinking air in one gulp. Toto is in one gulp. Truck has a beer, robot has two beers, bank has three beers, anode doesn't have anything. Toto has a beer of beer. Boss tells truck he is rid of sambon. Toto drinking a beer with boss, truck and sambon. Sambon takes his truck and leaves. A truck, a beer, an area, a pump. At the pump Robot pumps gas to fill a truck tank. Paying. Pictured fills it up by pumping until the tank is full. The truck makes the trip from the pump to the place for leaving the truck where it is while pictured goes leaving the truck alone. His truck is alone with the other lone trucks. Truck parks. Pump parks. Forgiveness parks. Payed is parked. Truck, Boss, Car, Payed have fun drinking a beer. Boss brings back the beers. There, payed drinks. The flowing current comes into play and connects up the pylons. Spoiled serves a beer. Boss knows spoiled. Sambon knows spoiled. Spoiled serves, plays server. Toto hasn't seen anything and hasn't heard anything. Toto swears he can't go any faster that he is at exactly the same speed, and that everyone neither wants to go faster nor slower that all is settled in at the same speed, Toto must have dosed all the speeds. Toto says we're fine that way. Toto has slowed down. In reverse. Toto doesn't know who has taken sides. Toto has taken off. Toto is already far when the scene blows up. Ate the whole tray at the café. He has been able to get away. Toto seems surprised to have been able to get away with such a good deal. For Toto had seen right in dosing. Two saddlebagged customs agents go across the highway bridge. Not a truck moves. The cars are moving. The cars pass on time. It is time. Toto doesn't move, waits for truck drinking a half-beer of beer. Pictured leaves his truck between the pump and there where everything is left in place to go to the restaurant. He enters the restaurant leaving his truck there. Toto approaches pictured. Toto asks pictured to take it. Pictured goes directly to the toilets. Robot slips himself one behind the shirt collar. Pictured and robot have a shirt with pants. Toto has overtaken pictured. Pictured has left his truck there while going to the W.C. in the restaurant entrance. Forgiveness parked sleeps. The backs of truck, boss, robot, anode. Truck waits before redrinking a beer. Truck waits for a beer. Pictured will come back. Truck doesn't ask, Toto doesn't ask. Boss doesn't ask. The direction is that in which the entire station goes. By the only passage through the area in the same direction. All the station and all beside the station and all the idiots are going in the same direction. Toto is the right dose. Toto stopped. Toto is just going to put himself in the right place. Toto is in the right place. He can dose now, now he doses. He hears all the places that move. When truck and pictured will set off in the direction the highway will leave from the station in the highway will quit the area. When the trucks will have been parked will leave again will leave again in the night or at daybreak. Toto waits to get in a truck, the truck belonging to pictured. Toto says not. Truck says nothing. Pictured pisses. Those who aren't driving are at the restaurant, or are in the restaurant entrance, forgiveness sleeps in his back in his truck. Truck doesn't answer. No answer is the right answer. Toto just waits. Toto watches pictured piss. Toto doesn't see truck not responding. Truck wants to drink. Pictured wants to piss. Truck drinks a beer. Boss says that Sambon's an idiot. Bank says that boss is an idiot. Truck says that sambon is an idiot and out of here. Boss clears out. Truck is late as usual. Toto is not in a hurry to leave. Toto is waiting for a night dose. Toto is waiting for a well-oiled beauty of a truck. With lights. Pictured makes his truck blink. Truck makes the head of his truck squeak. Bank has set off again by automobile. Car goes back to the garage just as anode does. Toto perfected a meter reader of dosed but unique doses of doses. Toto inventor of universal dosage. Toto and the unique doses. Truck doses, boss doses, the pump doses, the price has dosed. Toto, from the first refractory dose has perfected said new dose. The new dose is given like a second dose. And everything goes better. The second dose resolves the first dose. Toto measures the distance run between two doses. Toto gives a unique dose. Inventor of the measure of the first given. Toto has three highways. Toto has only one direction. Everything goes in the only direction. The bridges are not bridged. The rest area is oriented. Toto infers everything from underneath the bridge of the area. A Toto distance from the end of the area to the other end of the fencing enclosing the area. The enclosure of fencing. Toto will not take hours to finish the distance. The trip like everything is short is stopped. Toto is not going to the other end. The other end is normally there. Toto prefers coming back to the station. The night is dosed for just one dose. Toto wins at every stroke Toto wins breathes a good stroke. Has enough thigh muscles, muscled thighs, the muscles of thighs to be able to contain fate's bad strokes and get away running, upright if he must, Toto can get away running immediately. Toto doesn't run, Toto doesn't take flight. Toto stands his ground. Ah yes. Toto doesn't have a hole in the middle of his forehead. Toto's forehead has until then repelled all the bullets. Toto's forehead is bullet-proof. The middle of Toto's forehead repels all the bullets. Toto has a forehead that has repelled and that repels all the holes of the middle of forehead. Toto knows how to use his forehead to stop all hole bullets. No hole in Toto's forehead. Toto is left a bit of line. Doesn't escape into the country holding to all the trip done and the trip to be done. Toto is dead stopped. Toto has stopped in this station. He is in the station. There isn't only one area to stop in. Toto always goes straight ahead. He doesn't go back because he knows how to walk while remaining upright, walks upright, doses all of his steps to walk upright. To walk upright. Pictured holds his pisser to piss. Toto doesn't know what to do with his hard pisser. Toto arranges it as best he can inside his pants. It isn't so long. It is one line. Toto is all in one stroke and one mass and one line. Toto only has five segments. He doesn't lose his pants. Truck loses his pants. At the restaurant, they all eat to the brim. Toto hasn't payed, doesn't pay with pretense. Waits under the eighteen wheels, waits and counts the wheels, while passing in front counting Toto however has not payed. Toto doesn't deduct as he leaves. Toto gets out is a short line. Toto doesn't hold out. Toto doesn't hold out his hands. He is in all his height one line. Now, he takes part. Toto must take on. Toto takes himself on. Toto is not a load for rotor. He shows up already loaded, Toto is loaded. He shows up before pictured to leave with pictured if pictured wants. He hasn't answered, he answers no more than all the straight height of Toto. Doesn't hold himself out, shows up. Toto shows up with his dose, Toto is loaded dosed. Doesn't wait for nothing. As Toto is there he finds himself upright in the station. Being there he parks. The trucks park, boss parks, robot parks. It's not Toto who was killed. We know the name of the one who was killed. It's not Toto. It's. We don't know the name of the one who killed him, who left a mark on more than one life, a long life high up in the truck cab. It's a friend of Toto's who would kill Toto. Toto has four friends leaning on their elbows. The name of four friends. Four friends showing up before the question. The question remains upright. A friend is a back-up, kills you because you are a backup for your friend. Toto backs himself up. Toto did not kill himself. He was backed up, the bar counter was backed, the boss backs himself up and the transport is backed. Your friend is the one who will kill you. Toto looks at pictured. Pictured is Toto's friend. The friend of the killed is several last names. Killed has four friends and four friends of each of his friends. That's 20 friends. Robot meets one each time each one. Pictured isn't against it, no one's against it. Everyone rallies. It's the general rallying around killed. Anode says to boss one's hanging by the window. Everyone drives. The truck has remained open parked open to all the winds. Is filled with a lot of transport. All are into transport. The transporters gradually shoved in a lot of transport as they went. Toto shoves it in, the shoveler, must shovel in everything. Driver, pic-tured is the driver, truck is the driver. The driver has the keys to the door of the cab in the head that moves the trucks. Toto does not bear bad luck, bears bad luck to say the next time, Toto is a lucky charm. Because he bears luck. Bears attention at the entrance, remains beside the entrance, gazes at himself in the entrance. Toto has two white cheeks, two rounds of very white thighs, has an ass. Truck also has a big ass. Toto has lowered his pants. On the whole, in the rest area, only one will bear bad luck, the bad-luck charm. All maintain they are not bearing bad luck. Pictured has five lucky charms hanging attached. Boss has seen one dangling. From the suction mechanism that takes in a lot of air to the sealed compression of air. The tires are numerous. Bears attention at the entrance, to the map of the station, to the condition of the area or when rotor turns his truck. He makes it turn. The map of the station in his head. Toto has a head as big as his entire height and all the breadth of his two arms spread out-stretched, it's what thinks. The forms of rest areas, the directions of lanes, the forms of avenues, the path for going as far as the truck and making the truck turn. The truck turns because it has just the space. All the sta-tion what it is. It's useless to leave the highway. He who has killed is a friend of killed. Rotor doesn't make fun of Toto will not make fun. It's not insulting. It's not insulting Toto to not answer him to shut up. Pictured shuts up, rotor shuts up, robot shuts up. It's not lost effort. Toto's pressure and his dosage aren't dropping. Toto has just come dosed. Not speaking to Toto is not to insult Toto's honor in one go. Toto says can I go north with you guy. I'm going in the direction. Truck tow, window tow, safety tow. In the affair friend tow gets closer and closer to betrayal. I betray nothing, I'm not betraying being in friendship. I did not betray in killing him.

71

Killing. You have killed? Has lowered himself. Picks up what he needs to pick up. Friend tow is indeed the only one to pick up his stuff. Rotor is not Toto's brother nor all his family. Pictured is lived out. Is lived out for Toto. Toto should take the lived out of pictured. A lever, a steering wheel, a brake, a dashboard, a roller, a truck-bearer, a tire-wrench, a tire-lever, a notice, a sign, an amulet, a flag, an unjamming, a jam. Toto decides to climb without breaking. A single layer of all the clothing in the world, a single layer. Toto doesn't break, no breakage in Toto's lines. Take care of yourself we are the same. We are not the same. Toto needs a friend, a bear-er, a transporter. We all have our needs. Pictured is at the pump, pictured takes a pee, truck eats to the brim, he swallows everything. He doesn't need help to swallow everything, what he does. There are not several dosages. It's one by one by one. It's the main thing. Toto is lucky to be Toto. Knows he is. He never sets out with anything but all the luck on his side. He is sure he'll get right-side up again. At the height of Toto's honor. Toto is not too high. Toto at the sea. Toto in the sky. The luck Toto has to see the sky's grandeur. On the way up, the truck climbs and sees the sky big, he is half asleep as he climbs into the sky. Toto thinks I can't see where I'd go if it's not into the height of the sky. I don't see what I'm drawing myself up to if it isn't in the sky more vast than anything. Toto is upright. The events are monumental. Go well with a sky as vast as that. The sky plays the one who will escape but Toto won't be fooled. He doesn't leave with the sky that slides slowly with its weight to the right. Toto has it under his arms for it to jet, it has jets, it has a tendency to jet. He does it with his arms, thanks to the jets under his arms, he undoes all of the booby-traps. He does not undo his arms. He has shortened arms. He takes up in his arms what is in his arms. Loads his arms. Toto is a taker on who loads. He loads himself he is the one who knows how to load himself with doses to give and swallow. He swallows it. Toto presses his hard head against his only chance. And it's his only assurance. He doesn't know which head he has. He gazes at himself in the entry way. He knows the head he has, he's already seen it. He knows what pants he has. He saw the pants he had.

—*Translated by Jonathan Skinner*

Boxes (excerpts)

A cool place in the gray matter at the tender age of fresh and early morning, a fresh new corner in the gray matter in all the worn places a new refreshing renewal of the first rays of the sun of the day a renewal in a wrinkle of the brain in the freshness of a morning hour the rediscovery that there is still a real refreshing place in the old and hot worn gray matter the wrinkle in a year-old child's brain outside in the first gleams of day the intrinsic renewal of a crinkle in the brain providing the sensation of coolness of an entirely new place rediscovered, a newly refreshing part which had never been used which is located there hidden in the creases of a full used old hot brain, a small lively animal coming alive again in the gray matter, the gushing forth of a piece of the brain of a lively and fresh year-old child going outside early in the morning at sunrise.

The news flows over the head, the head loses shape with the arrival of the news, the truth slides over the head, flowing and falling on the head, the head melts, the features of the head drop, slide, the truth is slippery, the face is slippery, in realizing, the face slides, the news arrives and the head melts, all the features drop learning the news, the features melt, the news that comes flowing over the head like a truth makes consciousness slide realizing, makes the head slide, the head slides until under the features of the head that sink, melt, for the face, for the face, dementia, deformation, demonology immoderation mentality deformed outmodeable idea unde-formable indestructible discharge of flowing features shadow excess, courageously linked to the news, the news induces, the deformation is induced by the news slipping over the head onto the features up to the features of the head learning the news looking at it the transformation of the being is the face that loses shape from finding out something new news newly acquired by consciousness and conscience. The news has the power to deform the whole head.

The protruding top of the cage with holes, two hollows at the edge of the protruding pulp at the hind of the cage with holes, two round hollows at each edge, the end flexible, under the hump under the two hooded humps under the huge round whole under the huge whole, the huge round whole with melting pots, with humps, the huge hard hood of the flexible stem, the two holes in the harder humps at the edge of the flexible stem, holding the crease atop the flexible stem, the dampened soft crease, the digable dampened soft crease, under the whole, the hard boxed edge of the huge round whole hies over the huge whole, the two hollows and the two humps and the two pulps, and the lower hard edge of the block of the whole, the huge hood, the stem with a softer end, the dampened flexible crease, under the hard block of the under, the huge round hood, round going round to the other side, to the side of the two dug holes, of the two hard humps holding the flexible stem, the soft edges of the two humps, the whole soft half holding the four hard humps, a cage with holes with a huge hooded whole edged with a sealed hem under except for the wee soft damp crease.

Or you're on an enormous sphere, or you're fat on top of an enormous sphere, or you're on an enormous ball balanced on one leg, or you're drunk on top of an enormous sphere, or you're above all the way up at the top of a high balanced globe, or you're enormous on an enormous elastic sphere on only one leg, or you're on a large leg above up on an enormous globe, or you're fat drunk atop a sphere at the top, in the center of the top, at the highest spot at the top of a high globe, smack in the center, balanced on one leg on a long stretched out leg, fat in the middle, a big drunk in the middle, atop, at the top of a sphere, vertical, balanced, on a fat round ball, on an enormous round spherical ball, on the top of a very high sphere, on one leg, on a very high leg, or you're drunk on a globe, or you're drunk on a high globe, or you're up there without falling, or you're drunk by accident on one leg at the top of an enormous globe.

An ensemble of elements without elements, an ensemble of elements amassed, an ensemble made of elements without elements, an ensemble full of elementless elements, an ensemble of elements without even one element, an ensemble of elements without a multitude of elements, an ensemble that is elemental, the ensemble enough of an element, an ensemble that's enough, an ensemble of elements amassed, an ensemble set, an ensemble full of elements without an element, an ensemble without number, a full ensemble without number, a full ensemble without one, an ensemble of elements without getting one, an ensemble full of elements without giving one, an ensemble of elements without getting one out, an ensemble full of elements without having to have one, an ensemble made of elements in an ensemble, an ensemble of elements in one, an ensemble made of single elements, an ensemble of elements amassed, an ensemble with no other elements, an ensemble comprised, an ensemble with no other ensemble, an ensemble without another, an ensemble altogether, an ensemble amassed.

—Translated by Chet Wiener

hurt
a libretto

voice 1:
ouch, i hurt

voice 2:
she's in pain

narrator:
the pain has come over her and remains

voice 1:
ouch, i hurt
the hurt hurts me
i don't know what's wrong with me
i don't know why
but i hurt

narrator:
the pain settles in
it is pink or blue

it comes from far off and settles in
come to take hold of her
it holds her

voice 1:
i hurt
the pain advances comes to get me
i say ouch
i feel bad
ouch it would be better if it stopped

voice 2:
she hurts
the pain came

she received the pain
if she hurts like this that's because the pain came
where did it come from?

narrator:
amid that which is not there is pain
a persistent feeling
it came inside and it keeps

voice 1:
ouch i hurt
because of the pain
the pain's everywhere
i want it to stop, i want to go, i want to get rid of it

voice 2:
the pain came, what can she do, what she can do is
to hurt
she hurts
it won't let up

that i don't separate itself from
that i can't separate itself from

how did the pain suddenly come

narrator:
pain is an objective reality
pain must heal itself
it wasn't chosen and wasn't forewarned
it came on its own and overcame

voice 1:
i can't get rid of it
it's i who hurt
i'm painful

voice 2:
she houses hurt
hurt takes up the whole place
the place in the center

narrator:
pain settles in the center
and what's felt
is to feel

voice 1:
i have a feeling
a feeling that hurts and overcomes me
i don't have any other feelings

voice 2:
as if the emotion of pain were emotion, as if feeling pain were feeling, as
if you could no longer take away the feeling of pain without taking away
feeling, as if pain were only exactly what is felt, you feel? you want to feel?
i'm what you feel, i'm feeling, i'm all that can be felt, you're sensitive, you
hurt

narrator:
pain is in place in the part that feels
that must be felt, pain the need to feel all, don't ask,
you have to feel all
you are the need to experience everything
you are you must feel
hurt is automatic

voice 1:
i'm sensitive
i can't get rid of it
must have a feeling
i feel

voice 2:
i hurt, i think you hurt, i think i see that you're hurt, i think i under-
stand that for once you hurt, you don't know what to do

pain is simply, only, what came to feel itself

narrator:
the idea that it will end what feeling is to feel
what feeling has of pain hurts in insisting upon ending by chance

how to resist?
there must be some way to resist

voice 1:
i don't want it to stop anymore
i won't stop
confounding it

i want to survive

ouch i hurt
i will hurt

voice 2:
you have to think of something else or be something else that does some-
thing else or take it and push it farther to cry and joke or it has to para-
lyze but not me, pain came and paralyzed me, it paralyzes everything, it's
not me it paralyzes, it paralyzes me but i'm just ahead, to the side, just next
to, i see how it makes me suffer

narrator:
pain is just where it hurts
it hurts to have to feel
as if feeling were what has to

there's the possibility of resisting
of distancing

of getting rid of
here's how to distance the pain that drowns that will drown

voice 1:
i am a total block of feel
i feel feel feel
i can't do anything other than what i feel i feel

voice 2:
it's hard to weed out
the pain's in the middle
it went and took over the middle

narrator:
a fear, an illness,
an insistence, a preoccupation,

voice 1:
ouch i'm the hurt
i melt myself
i'm going

voice 2:
i want to go i want to get rid of it

narrator:
it says: i want to go, i want to get rid of it

voice 1:
it's mine, it's mine,
ouch i hurt
it's stuck how to pull it off

voice 2:
here's how it is to have so close close by
i've stuck it all over me

82

what stuck in coming came is hurt

narrator:
it is rare and unusual for a feeling to be so interior
that even the idea of asking it to go is absurd

voice 1:
i see no difference between me and i who hurt

voice 2:
it's the other, its' stuck,
limitless, took just one seat, settled in

narrator:
there is death, there are flowers, there is the moon, there is pain
pain that came and hasn't decided to go

voice 1:
i don't hurt anymore, i don't hurt, suffering doesn't hurt anymore, suffering is with me, i don't want to get rid of it anymore, i don't see why i would get rid of it, i live with the hurt, i am the hurt, i'm not too worn out, i'm holding on, i'll be the one who has the hurt inside

voice 2:
i'm going
i'm going to rip it out
i'll rip it out

narrator:
to feel it hurts

voice 1:
i hurt ouch ouch ouch
i'm me, i hurt
i'm me, i hurt

voice 2:
it'll go, it'll go
it won't hurt anymore

narrator:
no need to feel it
it is feeling itself

—*Translated by Stacy Doris*

TWO BORN

Bertrand Verdier interviews Christophe Tarkos,
November 3 1996—Paris, 13th Arrondissement

Bertrand Verdier: Two of your recent articles, one in Action Poétique, *the other in* Nioques, *explain your development somewhat, and might clarify the reading of* Oui, *especially regarding the "theory of worddoh," which begins* Oui, *in the "Poem of Outside."*

C. Tarkos: In any case, you are always obliged to use Worddoh; that is all you have. This book departs from worddoh. It's a little changed, staying in worddoh but a bit more lively. Obviously it's a little contradictory, there's a problem because in worddoh the lively doesn't lead far.

B.V.: The title Oui *supposes an acquiescence. Does worddoh constitute a means to arrive at affirmation, at acquiescence? The text will serve to arrive at an accord?*

C.T.: No. It's not a means to arrive there because you have the yes at the beginning. It's like the thrust of an umbrella; you need the thrust, the yes, in the beginning to make the worddoh smile. You can only make it smile; as it is somewhat elastic, you can enlarge it somewhat in a sense: that's all you can do. It's not much, but you try from the beginning to open yourself and to dance, to dance . . . In order to stir up the worddoh a tiny bit, you have to get a little wet. If not it doesn't move a millimeter. worddoh is a little like in demonstrations—I like this image of a herd—a demonstration is a totally malleable, suffocating positivity; you can't move it much; it moves very little and very slowly. That's exactly what you can do with worddoh: the emptier it is, the more useless. . . it's the mass that moves but that's all you can do, that's all. . . you need a good measure of yes . . . I'm thinking especially of the text *Le Compotier*, where the guy, the speaker, says, 'I'm joking.' The act of joking provokes fear, that makes the compote move, that makes vibrations. Laughter is very strange, in its origin.

B.V.: You speak of laughter, and on that subject, I was saying to myself that what you do with language, once you have this enormous mass from which you finally distance yourself, supposes a certain practice of irony, does it not?

85

C.T.: No there's no practice of irony. It's funny. It's the word that bothers me. When you have a cop who comes and tells you good morning and you tell him good morning, sir, that's not irony; or when you pay taxes. And in the texts of baroque opera, for example, could you say that there is irony? I have a problem with that, what is understood by irony - there is always a problem with that which one doesn't understand. People talk to me of formalism, I don't understand what they're talking about; for irony, it's the same problem; is the television irony?

Baroque opera texts are nevertheless bizarre when you read them.

B.V.: Still, your texts give an impression of distancing. It functions, it functions, and maybe they won't stop unless it stops working or it can only evolve into irony.

C.T.: Oh, I see. Okay. Because if it evolved into irony, it would be . . . I mean there's this joy and it absolutely must not turn into . . . into . . . I don't know how to describe it. In fact, I think that irony isn't very nice, as far as I understand. Because it's as if your work no longer existed. I was thinking of the distancing you mentioned; I can't write without it. By definition, writing is a real thing, an exterior thing. I think that bears upon irony.

B.V.: Your writing often begins with a simple sentence, you make language work, in the plurals, in the writing, the syntax. . . and progressively it seems to no longer be able to function.

C.T.: And then I stop.

B.V.: And then you stop. But you constantly give an impression of self-mockery, of being ironic in relation to what you're doing with the language, and somehow also in relation to the poetry in itself.

C.T.: But at the same time, everything takes place in my mind at a level which is neither technical nor linguistic. Raymond Roussel is not ironic; Fernand Raynaud is not ironic . . . I think that even if a guy wanted to be ironic, he couldn't, because the fact of wanting to be ironic means that there's a problem which is not ironic at all. I would say that even if there's an ironic aspect, it's only an aspect, the aspect that creates.

B.V.: In all your texts there's a side that's militant against inculcated, familiar language, but this denudification of the cogs of language makes it impossible to take language, as you use it, seriously—that's what I call irony; in showing how language functions, your text is hardly the more believable. There's a contradiction between the incredibility of language, which you demonstrate, and the truth that you claim to speak; isn't there?

C.T.: That's exactly where there is no contradiction. Something very strange, which always shocks me, but which afflicts me totally, is that people tell you that to tell the truth, you must make an attempt, have an instrument, language, which is perfect for that, really precise, straight as a die, you know, superfine, and in addition you can go anywhere with it because it works everywhere and therefore you use it to tell the truth. That makes me completely crazy, people who believe that. Whereas you just have worddoh, you know, you don't have much and you're really going to tell the truth with that. You're not going to use it to make an explanation, you're going to use it directly, poof, it's done, worddoh, that's your dish, that's the only dish anyway—the essential thing is that it be a true dish. That's the real poetry, poetry is always like that. And it's true that the remark you're making is exactly the kind of remark one makes when one thinks one can really make use of language to explain something. I was thinking about that the other day, I was thinking they tell you "There are people who deal with truth, they're called philosophers, and they speak the truth." But they make great poems. No one's going to use a philosophical text as a text that says something, otherwise you'd have a bunch of axioms. And therefore when they try to say the maximum possible of the truth, that makes a pretty unusable text, in the sense that it's the only thing you can do. It's neither clearer nor more useful than a poem. It's the same thing. Otherwise, it's pedagogy, immediately you're dealing with pedagogy and we know what that is, that it lies: but that's normal; that's its function.

B.V.: You say very clearly: "You see, truth be told, it's the poem . . . the poem doesn't reveal the truth of the world, but it reveals the truth." This truth, what is it?

C.T.: The problem with truth is that there are professional truth-tellers; a guy who uses other professional means under the guise of professional truth-telling's going to fail, in any case. That's really the collage between expression—between the letter, that which is written—and meaning. The only moment where it sticks is in the poem. That's why poetry's interesting, by the way. Otherwise, it would have no interest at all.

B.V.: And therefore you don't consider language as an obstacle to reaching the world, you don't give a damn about getting back to what is? Or else man speaks separate, as Prigent says, which he must have gotten from Lacan, who himself must have borrowed it from. . .

C.T.: From Fernand Raynaud, of course.

B.V.: You don't write yourself into this problem? You write in Nioques "the word is not a reference, is not a signifier, the word has no reference, is not two-sided, is not dual, is not sign."

C.T.: Yeah . . . they seem to believe words exist, I think that's just it; but for me, they don't . . . what I find strange about this idea is the fact that language and the world are separate. For me language isn't outside the world, it's as concrete as a bag of sand falling on your head, it's completely real, completely effective, efficient, useful.

B.V.: The solution you propose is, for example, to write on the word 'word'; you could have taken any other word than the word 'word;' you could have taken the word 'term' or the word 'sentence.'

C.T.: Yes, but it's even more flagrant with the word 'word,' and it's an even nastier lie, because the word 'chair,' you could say, well, we try to approximate it, more or less, to use a thing, sometimes you see what it is, sometimes you don't but anyway . . . So the word 'word,' the definition, you could say, is a lie in the pure state. The word 'chair,' you could say, means nothing; whereas the word 'word' is telling you: the word means something. They're telling a lie; it's no longer even an example of a lie, they tell you.

B.V.: In announcing clearly, "To tell the truth, uh-oh, that'll cause the revolution," you're dismissing a lot of contemporary writers.

C.T.: I have the impression, you could say, that my idea is dumb and nominalist—it rejoins something more virtual and at the same time old, there's a whole thread like that, since the nominalists of the Middle Ages . . . There's one part where I find myself in a contradictory position to them: on one hand, they say that world and language are separate and on the other, they say, if you change language, that will do us good. I find that a bit contradictory, because for me, language, it's like . . . it's hormonal. So basically it's true that the way you position it, with respect to the truth . . . It's not a philosophical thing, truth, it's therapeutic, medical, totally medical; a lie, that'll kill you someone. That's what you have to understand: you tell a man a lie, and all his life he's sick, and why? Because once there was a lie. That, like, has a reality on a verbal level; the verb is totally fleshly, corporeal, and more than being fleshly, it's like a gunshot. You can't say that language is separate at this moment, and, in addition to being a tool that way, a utensil, a bullet in the head, in addition, it's something concrete. But this relation to the world, it's true that when you change language, that changes everything, probably it changes everything. That's why the limit is so obvious, so close and physical. . .

B.V.: So you differentiate yourself from the literal, because you're more in the idea that there is an absolute truth to say, which is not a truth of what is, which is a truth without an objective complement. Is that it?

C.T.: Something I really like, that Jean-Marie Gleize said, is, "There is no double meaning." And the truth, for me, is the truth of the text. It's simply that everything is in the text. At a given moment, you said, "it's useful, the text is useful for something." Uh, no. The text is not useful for something, it is something. What bugs me every time is forgetting the materiality of the text. There is truth in the text, that's all, the palpable truth of the material existence of the text.

B.V.: Which is not a truth of something; the words have no referent.

C.T.: Yes, that's why it's not an absolute truth. It's more the vari/, the ver/, the verita/, the variety . . . the material variety of the printed. It's truly hormonal; the physical truth. If you say a word to a man and he's sick, or a word and he's better . . . you'll say, "yeah, but the word, does it have meaning, does it tell the truth, isn't it a twisted truth, is it. . ." who gives a shit! Nobody gives a shit! The fact is that this word has a physical effect.

B.V.: But one could always object that at that moment, your text is self-referential and therefore necessarily true.

C.T.: But at that moment, one is forgetting another thing, meaning. The thing is, it's stupid, but a word is linked to a sensibility in relation to what we call meaning, sense. Something even stranger is that on one hand, you can say, "your text is sufficient unto itself, it's pure materiality." But you always forget that any word, no matter which one, makes reference to the sensitive function of sense. So on one hand, this isn't an absolute truth, it's material, but a materiality always in relation to the sensitivity that you have for sense, which is after all physical. You can't say that it has to do with the formal problem, that means nothing whatever—unless you put incomprehensible signs, Chinese letters. That would be formal in relation to the image of the page. If you put any old thing, there's our sense-detector that panics, goes crazy, searches for something; it would search for something in everything, even in Denis Roches's *Dépôts de Savoir de technique*. We have, all of us, a working sense detector.

B.V.: Some of your poems are surprising in their length. "The Train," "The Spinning Wheel" and "I n't," for example, extend for several dozen pages. Can these still be called poems? Or is it that you arbitrarily stop them? Because they seem as if they could go on forever.

C.T.: Each poem is a gust of air, nothing else; "Zinc," for example, is the symbol of this little gust. The poet is made to arrive at a second, then a third poem . . . That's the difference between the poet and the madman; the poet is he who ends the poem.

—*Translated by Geneva Chao*

SELECTED BIBLIOGRAPHY

Calligrammes de Caen. Caen: École des Beaux-Arts de Caen. 2000.

Ma Langue (Three-book boxed set containing *Carrés, Calligrammes, Donne*). Romainville: Al Dante/Niok. 2000.

Pan. Paris: P.O.L. 2000.

L'Argent. Al Dante. 1999.

La Cage. Romainville: Al Dante. 1999.

Dix ronds. Martigues: Les Éditions Contre-pied. 1999.

Je m'agite. Hérouville, Saint-clair: Mir-X-presse. 1999.

Le Pot. Rouen: Derrière la salle de bains. 1999.

Le Signe =. Paris: P.O.L. 1999.

Caisses. Paris: P.O.L. 1998.

Le Bâton. Marseille: Al Dante. 1998.

L'Hypnotiseur soigne. Brussels: Éditions Secrètes. 1998 (with drawings by Pascal Doury).

La Valeur sublime. Toulouse: Le Grand Os. 1998 (with photographs by Larry Gianettino).

Farine. St-Étienne-Vallée-Française*: AIOU.* 1997.

Processe. Plombières-lez-Dijon: Ulysse Fin de Siécle. 1997.

Pupe. Le Mans: Muro Torto. 1997 (with a drawing by Balbino Giner).

Le Sac. Berguette: Station Underground d'Émerveillement Littéraire. 1997.

Toto. Bagneux: Encyclopédie des images. 1997.

Le Train. Berguette: Station Underground d'Émerveillement Littéraire. 1997.

Damier. St-Étienne-Vallée-Française: AIOU. 1996.

Expressif. Héronville, Saint-Clair: Aux Éditions Cactus. 1996.

Ma langue est poétique. Lyon: Electre. 1996.

Oui. Marseille: Al Dante/Niok. 1996.

Morceaux choisis. Arras: Les contemporains favoris. 1995.

L'Oiseau vole. Fontenay-sous-bois: L'Évidence. 1995.

In English:
"En plongeant un doigt dans l'eau." Trans. Jena Osman. *Raddle Moon* 16: 1997.

Excerpts from *Le Signe = .* Trans. Amanda Katz. *Germ 5*: 2001.

ROOF BOOKS

- Andrews, Bruce. **EX WHY ZEE.** 112p. $10.95.
- Andrews, Bruce. **Getting Ready To Have Been Frightened**. 116p. $7.50.
- Benson, Steve. **Blue Book**. Copub. with The Figures. 250p. $12.50
- Bernstein, Charles. **Islets/Irritations**. 112p. $9.95.
- Bernstein, Charles (editor). **The Politics of Poetic Form**. 246p. $12.95; cloth $21.95.
- Brossard, Nicole. **Picture Theory**. 188p. $11.95.
- Champion, Miles. **Three Bell Zero**. 72p. $10.95.
- Child, Abigail. **Scatter Matrix**. 79p. $9.95.
- Davies, Alan. **Active 24 Hours**. 100p. $5.
- Davies, Alan. **Signage**. 184p. $11.
- Davies, Alan. **Rave**. 64p. $7.95.
- Day, Jean. **A Young Recruit**. 58p. $6.
- Di Palma, Ray. **Motion of the Cypher**. 112p. $10.95.
- Di Palma, Ray. **Raik**. 100p. $9.95.
- Doris, Stacy. **Kildare**. 104p. $9.95.
- Dreyer, Lynne. **The White Museum**. 80p. $6.
- Edwards, Ken. **Good Science.** 80p. $9.95.
- Eigner, Larry. **Areas Lights Heights**. 182p. $12, $22 (cloth).
- Gizzi, Michael. **Continental Harmonies**. 92p. $8.95.
- Goldman, Judith. **Vocoder**. 96p. $11.95.
- Gottlieb, Michael. **Ninety-Six Tears**. 88p. $5.
- Gottlieb, Michael. **Gorgeous Plunge**. 96p. $11.95.
- Greenwald, Ted. **Jumping the Line**. 120p. $12.95.
- Grenier, Robert. **A Day at the Beach**. 80p. $6.
- Grosman, Ernesto. **The XUL Reader: An Anthology of Argentine Poetry (1981–1996)**. 167p. $14.95.
- Hills, Henry. **Making Money**. 72p. $7.50. VHS videotape $24.95. Book & tape $29.95.
- Huang Yunte. **SHI: A Radical Reading of Chinese Poetry.** 76p. $9.95
- Hunt, Erica. **Local History**. 80 p. $9.95.
- Kuszai, Joel (editor) **poetics@**, 192 p. $13.95.
- Inman, P. **Criss Cross**. 64 p. $7.95.
- Inman, P. **Red Shift**. 64p. $6.
- Lazer, Hank. **Doublespace**. 192 p. $12.
- Lazer, Hank. **Doublespace**. 192 p. $12.
- Levy, Andrew. **Paper Head Last Lyrics**. 112 p. $11.95.
- Mac Low, Jackson. **Representative Works: 1938–1985**. 360p. $12.95, $18.95 (cloth).
- Mac Low, Jackson. **Twenties**. 112p. $8.95.
- Moriarty, Laura. **Rondeaux**. 107p. $8.
- Neilson, Melanie. **Civil Noir**. 96p. $8.95.
- Pearson, Ted. **Planetary Gear**. 72p. $8.95.

- Perelman, Bob. **Virtual Reality**. 80p. $9.95.
- Perelman, Bob. **The Future of Memory.** 120p. $14.95.
- Piombino, Nick, **The Boundary of Blur**. 128p. $13.95.
- Raworth, Tom. **Clean & Will-Lit**. 106p. $10.95.
- Robinson, Kit. **Balance Sheet.** 112p. $11.95.
- Robinson, Kit. **Democracy Boulevard.** 104p. $9.95.
- Robinson, Kit. **Ice Cubes**. 96p. $6.
- Scalapino, Leslie. **Objects in the Terrifying Tense Longing from Taking Place.** 88p. $9.95.
- Seaton, Peter. **The Son Master**. 64p. $5.
- Sherry, James. **Popular Fiction**. 84p. $6.
- Silliman, Ron. **The New Sentence**. 200p. $10.
- Silliman, Ron. **N/O**. 112p. $10.95.
- Smith, Rod. **Protective Immediacy**. 96p. $9.95
- Stephans, Brian Kim. **Free Space Comix**.
- Tarkos, Christophe. **Ma Langue est Poétique—Selected Works**. 96p. $12.95.
- Templeton, Fiona. **Cells of Release**. 128p. with photographs. $13.95.
- Templeton, Fiona. **YOU—The City**. 150p. $11.95.
- Ward, Diane. **Human Ceiling**. 80p. $8.95.
- Ward, Diane. **Relation**. 64p. $7.50.
- Watson, Craig. **Free Will**. 80p. $9.95.
- Watten, Barrett. **Progress**. 122p. $7.50.
- Weiner, Hannah. **We Speak Silent**. 76 p. $9.95
- Wolsak, Lissa. **Pen Chants**. 80p. $9.95.
- Yasusada, Araki. **Doubled Flowering: From the Notebooks of Araki Yasusada.** 272p. $14.95.

ROOF BOOKS
are published by
Segue Foundation, 303 East 8th Street, New York, NY 10009
Visit our website at **segue.org**

Roof Books are distributed by
SMALL PRESS DISTRIBUTION
1341 Seventh Avenue, Berkeley, CA. 94710-1403.
Phone orders: 800-869-7553
spdbooks.org